COMMANDO HELICOPTER AIRCREWMAN

An account of the Military career of Warrant Officer 1 John Sheldon RN.

This story tells of WO1 John Sheldon's flying career of over 8,000 hours and 51 years of military service in the Royal Navy, Royal Air Force and the Royal Naval Reserve Air Branch of the Fleet Air Arm.

Joining the Royal Navy as a fifteen-year-old boy entrant in 1968 not long out of school, then recruited into the Fleet Air Arm as a junior electrician. Later becoming a commando aircrewman and flying in all types of service helicopters and in all of their roles. From first going to the evacuation of Cyprus during the Turkish Invasion in 1974, through Northern Ireland, the Falklands War, the Lebanon, and then on to the first Gulf War, Bosnia, Sierra Leone and then out to Afghanistan. He completed several tours as a Search and Rescue aircrewman, Anti-Submarine Operator and also as an RN/RAF Test aircrewman at the Rotary Wing Test Squadron at Boscombe Down.

It covers the military action in which John took part, the many incidents and close shaves he was involved in and about the friends he lost during his long and illustrious career.

The story of one man's fifty-one-year career as a
Royal Navy and Royal Air Force Helicopter Aircrewman

COMMANDO HELICOPTER AIRCREWMAN

51 Years in Action with the RN and RAF

John Sheldon

AIR WORLD

AIR WORLD

COMMANDO HELICOPTER AIRCREWMAN

First published in Great Britain in 2021 by
Air World
An imprint of
Pen & Sword Books Ltd
Yorkshire – Philadelphia

ISBN 978 1 39909 379 8

Typeset by SJmagic DESIGN SERVICES, India.

Printed and bound in the UK by CPI Group (UK) Ltd, Croydon, CR0 4YY.

Pen & Sword Books Limited incorporates the imprints of Atlas, Archaeology, Aviation, Discovery, Family History, Fiction, History, Maritime, Military, Military Classics, Politics, Select, Transport, True Crime, Air World, Frontline Publishing, Leo Cooper, Remember When, Seaforth Publishing, The Praetorian Press, Wharncliffe Local History, Wharncliffe Transport, Wharncliffe True Crime and White Owl.

For a complete list of Pen & Sword titles please contact

PEN & SWORD BOOKS LIMITED
47 Church Street, Barnsley, South Yorkshire, S70 2AS, England
E-mail: enquiries@pen-and-sword.co.uk
Website: www.pen-and-sword.co.uk

Or
PEN AND SWORD BOOKS
1950 Lawrence Rd, Havertown, PA 19083, USA
E-mail: Uspen-and-sword@casematepublishers.com
Website: www.penandswordbooks.com

Contents

Preface

The weather was cold, clear and blustery as we flew back at low level over Estancia having just delivered another external load of ammunition to the artillery battery near Mount Kent who were busy pounding the outskirts of Port Stanley. The first warnings came from my Aircrewmen John Sheldon and Alf Tupper who were keeping a close watch on the airspace astern. They had spotted two pairs of Argentinian Skyhawks who had popped out from the high ground behind us having just bombed the 3 Commando Brigade position. Unfortunately the enemy aircraft had turned towards us and had obviously spotted an 'opportunity target'. I was going flat out towards the cover of the high ground ahead and of course I was unable to see these enemy fighters that were attacking us from astern. Fortunately I could rely on my two exceptional aircrewmen who were steadily counting down the range and bearing of the fighters as they closed in on us. When the call come to 'break' I immediately threw the aircraft into a very steep turn and maximum rate descent, however I was very surprised to hear how loud the 20mm cannons sounded as the Skyhawks opened fire. I spotted a small ravine ahead and having recovered from our evasion manoeuvre I dived into that very narrow valley. Judging by the stream of warnings from John and Alf, they were quite surprised by the vigorous manoeuvring in a very tight valley but we had successfully evaded the fighters and were safe from a re-attack and with the Skyhawks on their way back to Argentina, we were able to find a space to land on and check the helicopter. Later we were reassured to learn that the Falklanders had named it 'impassable valley'!

13 June 1982 in the Falklands is still a very vivid memory for me but when you read John's account of this incident it sounds like fighter evasion was a fairly routine event. He does not mention the many flight hours spent training and then practising fighter evasion – or that the chance of survival of a helicopter when spotted and attacked by fighters in open terrain is very slim and that getting the right distance to break is absolutely vital. Breaking

vi

too early allows the fighter to adjust his flightpath to achieve the optimum aiming point and if you break too late you are also an easy target – you only get one chance and it must be right. Fortunately the experience and calm skilful judgement of John and Alf (and a bit of good fortune!) saved the day.

John Sheldon has had an amazing career as an Aircrewman and has built up a remarkable number of operational flight hours in a considerable array of helicopter types and roles. His skills have been built up and honed while serving for over fifty years in the Royal Navy and Royal Air Force, with the last few years before retirement in the reserves helping to train new aircrewmen and make best use of his invaluable aviation experience. Surprisingly he became a Naval Aircrewman more by luck than vocation – after leaving school at 15 he became an apprentice electrician but after only a couple of months, he found that very dull and as he was keen to leave home, he applied for the Royal Navy and was soon under training at HMS *Raleigh* down at Torpoint. He was volunteered by the system to be a Junior Electrical Mechanic (Air) and after initial training he was sent off to RNAS Yeovilton to learn his trade maintaining Sea Vixens and Phantoms. In 1971 he had two real strokes of good luck. Firstly he married Cathy and as they celebrate their golden wedding anniversary in April 2021 that was clearly a star move. John has been particularly lucky that Cathy was an ex Petty Officer WRNS and therefore well aware of the demands of service life and able to cope with the short notice operational deployments that John seems to have specialised in throughout his career! Secondly he was drafted down to RNAS Culdrose to his first Junglie (Commando Role) Squadron maintaining the Wessex Mk 5. 848 Naval Air Squadron introduced him to his first Aircraft Carrier, HMS *Albion*, and the joys of a Mediterranean deployment, and it was at this time that the first thoughts of becoming an Aircrewman appeared. Although he got little encouragement, he persevered and applied for the training, was accepted and soon got stuck into the basic flying training course which at that time had a worrying reputation for failing students. After a slow start John made the grade and he had his foot on the first rung of the Aircrewman ladder, a ladder which he would subsequently climb to the very top! His long career story covers flying many different types of helicopter and a variety of different operational roles – his chest-full of medals confirms that he has seen action all over the world and has been involved in virtually all of the hostilities that the Fleet Air Arm and the Royal Air Force has been deployed on in the last fifty years. Not only was he in the forefront of operational flying but he also played an important part in research and development flying during his years at the Aeroplane and Armament Experimental Establishment at Boscombe Down. He was also a particularly successful instructor who made a real effort to get his students to the highest standards. But perhaps his greatest accolade was his skill, intuition and crew cooperation which enabled him on several occasions to prevent his pilot from flying into the ground, sea or snow!

Foreword

In 2013, I was sitting in the Aircrewmen's Crew room of 848 Naval Air Commando Squadron at Royal Naval Air Station Yeovilton (RNAS Yeovilton). All the crewman were telling stories (DITs); I joined in and Buck Taylor, one of the instructors, said I should write a book as the DITs went on for quite a while, and the fact that I had been around the job for some forty-five years then (I joined in 1968) meant I had a few stories to tell.

So, I have decided to do as he asked and we'll see how it goes.

Foreword

Chapter 1

Going back to the start: it was 1967 and I was 14 years old. My family had just moved to Enfield in North London from north Norfolk. My father was in the RAF and he had just got a job recruiting in High Holborn, Central London. He had been in the Royal Navy during the Second World War; left for a couple of years then joined the RAF as a motor mechanic. This will be significant later on!

My mother was at home with my brother Paul. I was still at school and I never considered myself an academic of any sort, but did love playing around with engines and electrics, plus a bit of woodwork.

After a short while at the comprehensive school in Enfield, it became pretty evident to me that school was not the way ahead. I left school with no qualifications at all, but managed to get a place as an apprentice electrician at the British Electrical Resistance Company (BERC) in Ponders End, North London.

I started almost immediately after leaving school, which was in the new year of 1968. What a mistake. I soon found out that I was winding resistors on a lathe. The job was OK I suppose and the people were nice, but the same role of winding resistors all day, every day, was tedious.

There were men and women who had been with the company for years on end and had been doing the same job, over and over again for a lifetime. I looked on, and thought that my life has got to have more to it than this, as the Donovan song goes: 'Just get him to sign on the dotted line and work for 50 years.' Ohhhhhhhh No!

Combined with the drab job, home life was not great. My father drank too much and my brother, being eight years younger than me was mollycoddled by my mother, so I was always in the wrong. My sister, Ann, had married Geoff who was in the RAF, so she had escaped the family a couple of years before and was now living in Stafford.

So, I thought the same as a lot of young people who live at home and don't get on with their parents: I had to get away from my mother and father and live my own life.

1

Having been at the BERC for about three months, I made the conscious decision to join, or at least attempt to join, the military. I phoned the recruiting office in London and made an appointment, but with the Royal Navy not the RAF, where my father worked at the time. I was only 15, which was too young to join without my parents' consent, so I thought I would keep it quiet and not tell them what I was doing, until I got the go-ahead from the Royal Navy to join.

I went to an interview and applied to join as an electrician; the recruiters tried to convince me to be a chef – no way! I passed the interview and medical and a week later, got the letter telling me I could join, but had to get the form signed by my father. This was not a problem as my dad had shown no interest in my schooling nor what I did with my life, so I presented him with the form – he didn't even examine it, he just signed it. My mother wasn't too concerned either. Probably glad to get rid of me.

The signed form was sent off and two weeks later, I was informed that I had a place to join at HMS *Raleigh* in Plymouth just across the Torpoint ferry. I was to join on 30 September 1968; I would be four months short of my 16th birthday. I left home at the end of September; my parents didn't see me off, so I set off on the train via Waterloo Station to Plymouth. I was met by a petty officer seaman from HMS *Raleigh*, with about another twenty new entrants. A new part of my life had just begun, had I made the right choice?

There followed six hard weeks of basic training which included marching, weapons and seamanship training, and also covered first aid and the battle-damage course; this was carried out in a mock ship's compartment that either had water gushing in or a fire to extinguish. It was a simulator, but so realistic and a great experience which taught us to work as a team in hazardous situations.

I graduated at the end of the course but the Navy wanted to send six of the new entries to join the Fleet Air Arm. I had no idea what that was, we were shown a video of aircraft carriers and jet fighters taking off from flight decks. It looked quite busy and dangerous. We had all joined the Navy to go to sea as sailors, not to work on aircraft; surely that was for the RAF.

The choice was taken out of our hands; no one wanted to go, so they chose the top six from the IQ test that we had taken on joining *Raleigh*.

Fortunately, as it came to pass, I was one of those six and the direction of my life and career was changed completely. We were then sent to Lee-on-Solent, a Naval Air Station near Portsmouth to join the Fleet Air Arm, the air wing of the Royal Navy, where I became a Junior Electrical

Mechanic (Air) – or a WAFU (Wet and F---ing Useless) as the general service calls them.

I spent the next four months doing my electrician's trade training and was then sent to the Royal Naval Air Station Yeovilton in Somerset. I was now nearly 16½ and still really a young boy, but learning to grow up quite fast; I had to, I was working with some very dangerous equipment and alongside very able people who expected perfection and nothing else. If you got it wrong in those days, it was round the back of the hangar, a quick punch and learn the hard way. It happened to me once, but only once, I was a quick learner.

After training I joined 766 Squadron and qualified on the Sea Vixen Mk2 Aircraft, then moved to 767 Squadron and trained on the Phantom F4. I was so pleased I had ended up in the FAA!

It was the last week of December 1969 and I went to the Thursday dance on the camp; I was with a mate and ended up dancing with this rather nice girl, a little older than me maybe, her name was Cathy, she was a Women's Royal Navy Service Radio Operator (Wren RO) who came from Lancashire. I was still a junior who had to be in bed by 11.00pm, but I had a few drinks (even though I was under age) and forgot the time, when my Leading Hand came in and told me to get back to my mess deck. I made the excuse to Cathy that I was required to go to work ... not sure if she believed me.

Early the next year, I met Cathy again and after a while we started going out together, she was four years older than me and was about to be promoted POWRN; I was still a junior and a lot of people were amazed that we were together at all, considering the circumstances and age difference. We hit it off though and eventually I proposed to Cath and she accepted. We got married in the April of 1971 up in Adlington, near Chorley in Lancashire and Cath has been my rock and love ever since.

I continued to work on the Sea Vixen and Phantoms at the Naval Aircraft Support Unit (NASU) and got all of the aircraft qualifications I was required to achieve. On one occasion while working in a Sea Vixen engine compartment, I had to sort out the fire bottles which were electrically operated. The engines were out and I made sure the power was off, while I worked on the bottles. Unfortunately though, as I started on the bottles, another engineer came along and applied power to the aircraft. Sod's law also applied as the fire bottle buttons had been pushed in and stuck on. All this added up to the fire bottles operating as I was working on them. They went off straight into my face; I thought I had been blinded, I could see nothing and was rushed to the sickbay/medical centre and had my eyes washed out. I was not happy, but the Doc said I should be OK in a couple of days – he was right and I was able to see again the next day. The medication I had been given though dilated my pupils, so for the next two weeks I was walking round looking like Stevie Wonder, sunglasses day and night, because the bright light was killing me. But at least I would retain my sight.

At the time Cath and I lived in a caravan on the site just north of RNAS Yeovilton. A small van with no heating apart from an electric fire, and in the winter it was bloody freezing; so cold, in fact, that the water in the bowl of the toilet froze. But in the summer, it was great and the neighbours, John and Dianne were a fantastic pair.

At the end of 1971, I was moved to RNAS Culdrose in Cornwall to work on Wessex Mk5 helicopters, and at the beginning of 1972 I joined my first Junglie (commando) unit, 848 Naval Commando Air Squadron (NACS) based on HMS *Albion*, a commando aircraft carrier. I enjoyed the squadron and my time on there, the work was hard and the runs ashore were great; in fact, sometimes too good!

I was granted shore leave in Famagusta in Cyprus; we had been at sea for quite a while and I went ashore with Paddy Green, a fellow engineer on 848 Squadron, and a couple of other guys. Like young fools we drank too much, ending up on the local brew (ouzo) which was a form of Anisette – loopy juice. I drank a couple of small bottles and as we walked out of the bar, the air hit me and a few seconds later I was on the floor half-unconscious. At that moment I didn't know what was happening, but two Royal Marines picked me up and we all got a taxi back to the pier near Dhekelia barracks, where the lads let me go. I had drunk so much I didn't have any awareness of my surroundings at all and kept on walking … straight off the end of the pier and into the Mediterranean. Luckily the crew from the landing craft dived in and lifted me out of the water, otherwise I would have drowned (Life No.1). On getting back to the ship I was put in sick bay for my own good.

Next morning, I was right as rain, but the punishment was yet to come. The doctor said if I ever did it again, I would die from alcohol poisoning, and the commander at his discipline table gave me ten-days punishment and three-months privilege leave. Privilege leave meant I was not able to go ashore for three months without the commander's permission. To this day, I don't know why I was so foolish and have never touched a drop of anything like ouzo again.

I found working on the Wessex 5 was not as demanding or complicated as working on fixed-wing jets, so I lost a little enthusiasm for the job. I was considering my options when I saw these guys flying in the back of the commando helicopters and thought I would like to try it and give my working life a bit of a boost. So I put in for the course, and after going on the senior pilot's table, where he said he 'thought that I would never make it', he agreed to send me off. I would still have to get promotion as an electrician, but would work as an aircrewman.

By November 1972 I had completed and passed the interview, medical and survival test, all three of which were quite demanding, especially the survival test in the winter in the New Forest. We had to spend the night out, each in a one-man dinghy on a lake. To get out into the middle of the lake to inflate the dinghy, we had to break through the ice that had formed on the surface, wade out through the ice and then get into the inflated boat. Wet and cold, we then had to survive the night sitting on the water. By the morning I was very cold, still wet and glad the night was over. The only problem was that we had to get off the lake, so it was back into the water to drag the dinghy – which was to be my waterproof coat and sleeping bag for the next ten days – back to shore. It taught me to utilise all the available kit that I could lay my hands on in a survival situation. I was teamed up with Pete Jays and we had got a rabbit for food; he would not kill or skin it, or even cook it. But funnily enough, he was quite happy to eat it!

We then started our Basic Flying Training (BFT) on 771 Search and Rescue (SAR) Squadron at RNAS Portland, flying in the Wessex Mk1 SAR Aircraft, this was the start of the real training. It was now that I could prove the senior pilot of 848 Squadron wrong about me – which I knew was going to be difficult as the failure rate on BFT was about 70 per cent at the time.

This course consisted of Dead Reckoning Navigation, winching and winchman training, medical and survival training, meteorological and maths work, combined with all other sorts of aviation training. It was a difficult course and I passed, not with flying colours, but a pass is a pass. The instructors did a great job, Jan Greener was the boss in charge, Mick Crumby and Carl Fairbrother were our main instructors. Good guys, but very hard to please!

On completion of BFT at the end of January 1973, all the students were split up. Pete Jays went to Anti-Submarine Warfare (ASW), John 'Speedy' Ball went to Search and Rescue (SAR), Jim 'Slim' Freelove and I were going commando flying. We joined from BFT and met up with Joe 'Derby' Allen, an ex-SAR crewman to make up number 59 course on 707 Squadron at RNAS Yeovilton, where we began Operational Flying Training (OFT). OFT would be flown in the Wessex Mk5 that I had worked on while I was on 848 Squadron at Culdrose. The training would get more and more demanding, there was nowhere to hide on this course. Our instructors, PO Eddy Hughes, LEM(R) P.J. Spearman and PO Bob Niblock, worked us hard and long. The course involved lots of low-level flying down to 10ft at times, working with the pilot to navigate to pinpoint grid references in the middle of Dartmoor or Exmoor; this would be under a tactical situation, with enemy all over the place firing imaginary missiles and weapons at you. Good training that would save my life later on in my career. Later, we even had Royal Marines in the back and they would be involved in the tactical landings and exercises that we carried out.

We learnt how to abseil and rope out of helicopters, fire weapons such as the Air Mounted General Purpose Machine Gun (GPMG) from the cabin; all this during the day and then also at night. The end of the course culminated in a week-long exercise, ours was in Detmold in Germany. This was an exercise involving lots of troops and aircraft in a big tactical exercise environment. It involved a lot of troop moves, gunning, fighter evasion, day and night flying, while we were living in the field (i.e. under canvas). This was the make-or-break exercise; if you failed this week, then it was back to being an electrician on 848.

Luckily, the week went quite well – there was only one dodgy point: we were roping ten soldiers out from 50ft and one guy managed to slip off the rope 10ft from the ground and broke his ankle, the next flight was to the medical centre. It happens and would happen again, lots of times; it's a dangerous business.

At the end of the week, the exercise was complete and we were all called in for our final interviews. Happy days! We had all passed the course and on return to Yeovilton we would get our wings from the Captain of the Air Station (every one called him 'Captain Kodak', because he was always having his picture taken by the press or appearing on TV). Nice guy though, and it was great getting my wings. The extra benefit was that I also got extra pay – a whole 65p per day of flying pay!

We had two weeks leave then joined our first front-line squadrons as aircrew, Slim went to 848 Squadron; Derby and I joined 845. At that time, 848 was the warm weather unit and 845 covered the northern flank, which meant we would be going to Norway each year to fly in the Arctic for the winter; I was looking forward to that! Both squadrons went on commando carriers and did the same sort of flying role, just in different environments. The training had finished, but as anyone will tell you, that's when the learning really starts, when you get to the front-line and start doing operational flying; the real flying, the real thing.

Chapter 2

When I finally joined 845, it was like a breath of fresh air. I had finished training and the release was great. I was able to go home and see Cath each night while we were at Yeovilton. Obviously we would do time away, but when at home it was good. Cath was still in the WRNS at Yeovilton and she had been promoted to Petty Officer just prior to us getting married, which meant she was senior to me and got paid more, so not only was I her toy boy, but I was also a kept man! Life was good. We were still living in our caravan, but making plans to buy our first house; I had just turned 20.

Over the next few months, Derby and I worked really hard to establish ourselves as qualified commando aircrewmen. The qualification is achieved by completing all the tasks required in that role, which meant doing all tasks needed to support a commando unit from the Royal Marines. There were five main units, 40, 41, 42, 45 Commando and the main support group and all the other units including the SBS, SAS and plus any Army unit we were required to work with.

When we eventually had achieved our Certificate of Competency (C of C) we felt we had achieved a great deal, but still had to gain more experience in the commando role. Once we had our C of C, then we could really call ourselves 'Junglies'. The term came from the late 1950s and early '60s, when the commando squadrons operated in the Borneo jungle, supporting the troops during the Borneo Conflict. A term of endearment from anyone who has worked with us, and a name to be proud of.

Halfway through 1973, Cath and I bought our first house, situated in a small village called Bower Hinton, near Martock in Somerset. It was a terraced house with two bedrooms, fairly modern, no heating, but we soon sorted that out (no more freezing toilets for us!). We put gas heaters in and a gas fire in the living room. The neighbours, Carol and Charlie, were really nice people and they helped a great deal when I was away.

COMMANDO HELICOPTER AIRCREWMAN

During the remainder of the year, I was abroad or at sea on HMS *Hermes*, an ex-fixed-wing carrier, that had been converted to a commando carrier. 845 was the first Wessex Mk5 Commando Squadron to embark and we helped work up the crew of the ship. At that time, we had twenty-two Wessex Mk5 and one Wasp helicopter. The other flying units on board which made up the Air Group were 820, which was an Anti-Submarine Warfare (ASW) Squadron flying the Sea King Mk 2; and 3 Brigade Air Squadron (Royal Marines) at the time flying Scout Helicopters – they were always called 'Teeny Weenies' because they flew such small aircraft.

My flying career had been good, but quite uneventful with only minor incidents, which I supposed was the way life would be. Flying in helicopters can be quite hazardous; as most people who know about engineering are aware, the helicopter comprises thousands of bits of metal, whirling round, all at different speeds and in alternate directions, sometimes not all in unison and at times things go wrong! Sometimes the mechanics of the aircraft can go wrong, or if you are prone to carelessness and fly the thing in a cowboy-like manner, accidents will happen!

And so it was to be, the squadron was involved in an exercise in southern Norway; it was mid-year and the weather was nice with quite a strong northerly wind. When a conventional helicopter (main rotor with a tail rotor) is flying an approach into a landing site, it should be flown into wind and with a steady descent to the final hover/landing point. On this occasion we had ten Royal Marines in the back, I advised the pilot where the drop-off point was and he acknowledged the landing site. Unfortunately, between us and that point there was a set of 200ft-high power cables and instead of coming around the cables and making a steady descent into wind, the pilot threw the aircraft round, up over the cables, and lowered the collective lever, losing height rapidly and approaching the landing point downwind, which was not a good idea. I called for the pilot to overshoot, which he should have done, but he ignored me. On that, we started to drop like a stone and the aircraft entered a condition known as 'Vortex Ring'.

Vortex Ring occurs when an aircraft is descending with a high rate of descent at low speed. Recirculation of the air is set up around the rotor disk which causes the aircraft to descend faster, and to a point where it can't be recovered. Our aircraft was heavy and at low speed, plus we were downwind which made things even worse. There was only one way we were going and that was down. Below us was water. I shouted to the troops 'BRACE, BRACE', it happened so quickly that all of sudden we were on the surface of the water and starting to sink. With the impact of the airframe on the surface, the water had washed in a great wave over the engine intakes and into the cabin doorway, but to our amazement we didn't sink. Luckily for us, we had landed in a bog rather than a lake; it was about 3ft deep and the aircraft had hit the bottom and cushioned our impact. Because the weight had been taken off the rotors as we hit, the rotor speed had regained and – to everyone's astonishment – we lifted into a low hover, without the engines flaming out, due to the water ingestion when the aircraft hit the water.

Everyone was shaken but OK, so we moved over to the side of the bog and disembarked the troops. I asked the pilot why he had not overshot, because he could have killed us, but he said nothing. We decided to go back to our Forward Operating Base (FOB) and examine the aircraft. On inspection, the underside of the helicopter was full of puncture marks from the stones and vegetation in the bog.

I was still fuming that I had been ignored by the pilot and I needed to say something to someone in charge, because the pilot was still saying nothing to me. At that point one of my colleagues, Steve Huxley, who had been flying the same mission and watched our incident came up to me and said: 'John, I thought you had ditched and gone under when that happened, the engine intakes were totally under the water.' I told him what had happened and we came to the decision that I should go to the senior pilot and make plain what had gone on. The pilot had no defence, but still argued the case. Others watching the incident said he didn't have a leg to stand on. The senior pilot gave him a rollicking and told him that we fly as a crew and he should listen and react to all suggestions, commands and ideas. If it happened again he would ground him. After that incident, I didn't fly with that pilot again in any solo missions, just when there were two pilots up front.

On return home, all was good again. We had a couple of weeks leave then off again on board to do some amphibious training in Scotland. We returned late November 1973.

The programme for the next year was published; we were to have a long deployment. A few of us would leave before the new year to go to Norway, three months there and then go on board HMS *Hermes* for a six-month trip to the Mediterranean and Canada, before coming back in October 1974.

Cath was not happy when I got home and told her; ten months away was a long time and the longest we would have been apart. Secretly, I thought it was a long time too, but I was looking forward to Norway and getting my Arctic Warfare Training Qualification, which was the only part of my C of C that needed finishing.

We did all of our pre-Norway training/lectures/kit Issue and then departed for Norway. The aircraft were flown to Marchwood near Southampton, where engineers craned them onto an LSL (Landing Ship Logistic).

I was to go to Norway on RFA *Sir Geraint* with Petty Officer Tim Kelly, my fellow flight aircrewman to do our Arctic ground and flying training and we embarked on 30 December 1973, three days before my 21st birthday. As it would take nearly four days to sail to the north of Norway, my birthday would fall at sea; what a place to become 21 – the middle of the North Sea! The winds were gale force and the sea was as rough as I had ever experienced; I didn't throw up, but a lot of the guys did.

The ship prepared to come alongside in Norway, where the jetty protruded out from the small fishing town of Sorreisa; at the shore side of the jetty was a wooden house, built in the standard Scandinavian style. When the ship started its approach to dock it was going a little too fast; as we stood on the deck, we watched the ship got closer and closer then, as if in slow motion, it failed to stop and the bow of RFA *Sir Geraint* went straight into the bedroom window of the house. When it came to a halt, about 10ft of the bow was in some poor Norwegian's front bedroom.

Eventually we got to Royal Norwegian Air Force Base (RNAFB) Bardufoss, where the Arctic Training Cell (Known as the Clockwork Cell) was based. We would live there for the next three months. The temperature was about -20°C, the coldest I had ever experienced. We started our training, survival and acclimatisation. The flying was great, once you got used to the freezing cold. Mountain flying, landing with one wheel on the top of 8,000ft peaks, landing on ice/snow covered lakes, plus landing and load lifting in recirculating snow, which is a skill on its own. The survival was special, it took place on the German airfield which was about 5km east of Bardufoss.

Tim and I were paired up; we had to ski out and then fend for ourselves for four days/three nights. During the day it was about -15, but at night it would be -20 or less. We were given a reindeer skin and good sleeping bag to survive, but not a lot more. In the Arctic you have to get under shelter as soon as possible. So, Tim and I started to build a snow and wood shelter. We had a wire saw and a machete, which was OK; after about three hours hard work, we had our survival area complete. A shelter with a snow wall in front of it which was a perfect windbreak. The snow wall also reflected all the heat and light from the fire, we started cooking some powdered soup that I had managed to stash away before being searched. Melting some snow with the powder gave us a bowl of nice hot soup that was heart-warming and really comforting. The night was like no other, I had seen the northern lights before, but this night was so clear and bright. The northern lights were all over the sky, not just green, but full of colour. Nowadays I would use my camera to take some video, but back then we had no smart phones, so that evening sky is just a fantastic memory that will live with me forever.

The Arctic flying training started, it was good, but I remember coming back to the German airfield once more when we were carrying out troop drill with the Norwegian Army. I had already landed (Tim was in the second aircraft) and I was briefing some young Norwegian troops who had never flown before. I explained how the aircraft lands in a cloud of snow and that the troops use themselves as a marker for the pilot to land the aircraft against (i.e. put the front right wheel next to the troops as reference point for the pilot to see, so he does not get disorientated). They were fine with this until Tim and Chris Warne started their approach and the snow cloud built up behind the Wessex; as he slowed, the cloud started to overtake the aircraft with the down wash from the rotors. The cloud consumed the aircraft and we lost sight of it. The noise of the Wessex coming in was very loud, but all of a sudden the noise stopped. Instantly I knew there was something wrong and as the snow cloud gradually cleared, there was the aircraft, at a jaunty angle of about 45 degrees on the ground, front left wheel strut broken, both engines flamed out and rotors stopped.

I went over to the aircraft, both Tim and Chris were OK. The snow had engulfed the intakes and stopped the engines. The aircraft would be out of service for some six months, but did fly again later. More than I can say for the troops; after witnessing this they refused to fly, even though we still had one more serviceable aircraft. About two days later though, we managed to convince the army that all was OK and we managed to get all the troops flying and completed the troops' drills.

Of course, it was not all work; the runs ashore were quite good. Norway is very expensive though, so we would have a few drinks at the base and then go out. If you stowed away a hipflask full of your favourite spirit, a glass of water being topped up from your hipflask could last you all night. The skiing was also good, I was playing a lot of rugby then, and to keep fit I started running, but the roads were too icy. I saw some Norwegians doing cross-country skiing around some tracks during the day and a lit track at night. I tried my Pussers (military) skis first, but they were too wide for the tracks, so I managed to buy some langlauf skis and started doing cross-country skiing, what a great way of keeping fit.

On completion of our Clockwork training, it was on to exercise time, with the Royal Marines from 45 Commando. This took place in a tactical environment, which meant we all operated in the field, the Royal Marines in snow holes and bivouacs and us operating from FOBs supporting them. The exercise lasted two weeks, the temperature never got warmer than -23°C and -30°C at night, but if you're trained for the cold you can still work and operate in those very severe conditions.

When the land exercise had ended, we packed up all our gear into the aircraft to await HMS *Hermes* which had sailed from Portsmouth a week before and was coming up to collect us. A day later we embarked for one final exercise, then we would be off to the Med.

Back in those days the Wessex would fly single pilot only during the day, normally two at night. But sometimes, if a check test flight was required, it could be done single pilot at night. On this occasion the night flying programme was quite heavy and the squadron needed another aircraft. A crew had been nominated to go off and do what was called a PPI (Power Performance Indication Check) to see if the engines were working to the max. It was the night of 19 February and an Army exchange pilot called Captain John Greig AAC had been nominated to fly the aircraft. The crewmen were debating who needed to night fly. First Charley Hope, one of the three Able rate aircrewmen on the squadron, was nominated, then Tim Kelly said he needed to fly and finally David 'Taff' Evans, who was an aircrewman SAR diver, said he had the fewest night flying hours and needed to night fly to remain current at night operations. Captain Greig and Taff took off, into the cold Norwegian night sky. The process of the flight was to climb to 1,000ft to do the check, the pressure setting on the altimeter then had to be set at 1013 millibars (the standard pressure setting) so that the engineers could calculate the figures when the aircraft returned. We presumed that the PPI was carried out and the aircraft was returning to the ship. They were on their final approach when the helicopter flew straight into the sea at 90 knots (about 110 mph). Naturally everyone assumed that the pressure setting on the altimeter had not been reset to the local setting and as the pilot could not see the surface, he must have flown into the sea, the altimeter would have shown the incorrect height above the surface.

The exercise was put on hold and all the search and rescue drills were put in motion. We had been in the mess deck drinking our daily ration of three small cans of beer when we got the shout. We were all airborne and searching for the crew within twenty minutes. The night was as black as coal dust. All areas were searched, but in those day we had no night-vision aids or thermal camera, so we fired flares out of the back door; I had been

CHAPTER 2

sitting in the doorway for about thirty minutes when I suddenly became aware that my safety harness was not on and I was not strapped in to the aircraft. I slowly shuffled back to the safety of the cabin floor and put my harness on. It was bad enough to lose one crew that night, let alone another crewman. After that night I learnt another lesson: never drink before you fly. It's illegal now, but then it was accepted.

Wreckage had been found, it was the wheel, tyre and support leg from one side of the Wessex, there was also some other floating debris. The water temperature was about 3°C, so even if they had survived the impact, they would not have lasted long in to the night. It was a great loss, and it brought back to me how dangerous this job could be and as with most accidents, it happens when you least expect it. The whole squadron was gutted to have lost dear friends.

At breakfast the next day we started to queue at the servery, still in our immersion suits as we had been airborne all night long searching for the two crew. Behind the hatch of the servery there were two chefs, an AB and a Leading Hand. At the front of the queue was Ron Arscott, one of the crewmen. On getting to the servery the AB Chef said, 'At least that's one less crewman to feed.' We all went loopy, Ron was just about to climb over the hatch and kill the chef when the Leading Hand Chef grabbed the AB and laid him out with one punch. It was the right thing to do, because if we had got him, he would have been far worse off. We thanked the Leading Hand Chef.

The funeral took place a couple of days later on the back of *Hermes*, even though we had not recovered any of the bodies, and it was the first time I had ever cried for the loss of a friend and fellow aircrewman; it would not be the last.

The mood was quite sombre after that incident, but life goes on and we continued working hard, which I think was the best thing to do to get over our loss of friends and workmates. We sailed a few days later on the way to Hamburg, and during the following week a diving search ship came out to the crash site. It discovered Taff's aircraft lying about 360ft below the surface; we were told that the recovery team had tried to lift it from the seabed on the bottom of the fjord, but the aircraft had broken up in the attempt, hence the bodies of the crew were never recovered.

The whole squadron had now embarked on HMS *Hermes* and we were due to be on the ship for the next six months. After a run ashore in Hamburg, the ship set sail for the Mediterranean. As it happens, a ship's rugby match had been organised against Portland Naval Air Station on the south coast

13

in Dorset and as we sailed passed Portland, two Wessex from our squadron lifted from HMS *Hermes* and took us ashore to play the match. We were only there for two hours because the ship was still sailing west, but it was great because Cath and a couple of other wives had found out about the game and made the thirty-mile journey to Portland to see us. It was great to see her as I had been away for three months already and looking at another six months away; we had a quick kiss and cuddle, then off again. She told me later that the parting was worse for her: I was going back on board ship, but she was returning to an empty house.

The trip across the Bay of Biscay was quite uneventful, a bit of day and night flying. We turned east from the Atlantic into the Med and stopped at Gibraltar for a couple of days.

The next few months consisted of exercises around the Med and a few runs ashore in Malta, Southern Sardinia, Italy and Greece. The trip was going great, everyone was getting a good tan and we played rugby in each port, normally with the exiles from various other countries. These exiles always knew which was the best bar in town or where to go for a good night out after the match.

Then there was a change of plan. A flight of two aircraft were to go on board HMS *Fearless* an LPH (Landing Platform Helicopter), that would mean two crewmen would leave the ship and continue the detachment away from *Hermes*. Tim and I were chosen and Lieutenant Al Davis was the detachment commander. Al was a really nice guy and alongside him would be Sub Lieutenants Baker, Jones and Tweedy.

Yet again we packed up, left *Hermes* and embarked in *Fearless*, which was also the Dartmouth training ship. The *Fearless* was slightly different from *Hermes*, a much smaller ship, more intimate, so it wasn't long before we knew all the crew and became part of the ship's company. After one trip to southern Italy the ship put into the Bay of Taranto. During the Second World War this had been the scene of the destruction of the Italian fleet, by the Fleet Air Arm. Fairey Swordfish, nicknamed 'Stringbags', flew from aircraft carriers at night and destroyed the Italian fleet using torpedoes, dropped from underneath the belly of the Swordfish. It was a heroic raid that goes down in Fleet Air Arm history and is celebrated each year. While there we were given leave to have a beach BBQ, in the Navy it's known as a 'Banyan'. We had lots of wine and food, but the locals didn't appreciate this too much. Not anything to do with history, but because we were a group of young lads on their beach having a good time, in high spirits and probably very noisy. At the end of the afternoon, we made our way back on board, with all our kit. *Fearless* had backed on to the beach, which it could do because it was a docking ship. On leaving the ship the rule was that ratings (i.e. lower deck, not officer or senior ratings) had to leave their station cards in a box to prove they were ashore, so on return you had to recover said card. On my return, having had a little to drink and slightly worse for wear, I was carrying a body on my shoulder, not a dead one, but definitely one worse for drink. It was the flight commander Al Davis, he had drunk an awful lot of the local wine that afternoon and had passed out. As I approached the ship's stern I asked the duty petty officer for my station card; he gave it to me then asked who I had on my shoulder. He was just about to create hell when I informed him it was the flight Lieutenant Commander Al Davis. As soon as he found out it was an officer he changed his attitude. I said I would put him to bed and make sure one of the other officers looked after him. That is the routine, you look after your own, it goes without saying. As I had been looked after a few years before in Cyprus!

The trip continued around the Med, Izmir and Istanbul in Turkey, Northern Egypt, Greece again and then back to Malta. We were in Malta for three weeks, of which two was annual leave. Tim and I had asked if we could bring our wives out and the boss agreed we could. So, Cath and Steph came out for two weeks. It was a great escape from ship life and a really good holiday. We had a couple more exercises to complete on sailing from Malta, then it would be back via Gibraltar, through the Bay of Biscay and to the UK.

I arrived back home around the middle of August 1974; it was great to be home after almost nine months away. Most of all it was great to see Cath again.

Then the bombshell hit; a phone call about 7pm from the support unit at the squadron base in RNAS Yeovilton. All he said was, 'Don't unpack your kit, as you are being picked up at 0700 tomorrow morning to fly out from RAF Brize Norton in a Transport Aircraft to Cyprus to join HMS *Hermes*.' I was not impressed and Cath was even more upset, but at least I had one night at home. That was more than the guys on HMS *Hermes* had achieved.

Cyprus had been invaded by Turkish forces and HMS *Hermes* and the embarked commandos (41 Commando) would carry out an evacuation mission of all British passport holders, either to southern Cyprus or to the ships in the local area.

The next morning, I said goodbye to Cath again, she was really upset as I departed for Brize Norton, the main Transport Aircraft base for the

RAF. That afternoon, I was in the air and on my way back to HMS *Hermes* and the Med. As soon as we arrived back on board everyone was getting ready to fly. The first evacuation was from Mount Troodos, an RAF outpost and radar station and the highest point in Cyprus. Turkey had invaded the northern part of the Island, so everyone anywhere towards the north, had to be evacuated.

I was flying with a pilot called Lt Brian 'Bullets' Bellingham (so called because he was a Helicopter Weapons Instructor (HWI)). As we were flying towards Troodos, there were small explosions below us, we were at about 500 feet, so we climbed slightly. Never having been shot at before, this was a new situation and experience for me, and even for Bullets. The rounds kept on coming in, getting closer and louder, but we managed to get to Troodos OK, without any damage!

On arriving at the landing point, we carried out a confined area landing, as it was quite small landing site and just fitted a Wessex. At Troodos there was a marshal who was controlling the landing point and the evacuees, we could only take ten people at a time, due to weight restrictions, fuel and the number of seats available. The doors and windows had been removed to give us more capability, but even so that was all we could lift. There were workers' civil and military and families waiting to get on the aircraft. I got ten on board and tried to brief them over the noise, it was quite difficult as they were scared.

A family of four were the last to get on, they strapped in and we took off. A girl of about 12 years old was the last on and sat near the doorway, the door had been removed, so the wind was blowing straight onto her. With hindsight I should have put an adult there as I could see the girl was petrified when we got in the air, but it was too late – I could not move her, so I tried to comfort her. That didn't help though and she started to wet herself; I felt powerless to help her and her father sitting next to her was getting soaked by the flow of her pee. Lesson learnt! I vowed that the next time I had to do anything like this, I would plan the seating arrangement a little better.

Next job was to evacuate some children from Northern Cyprus. This was at sea level so more power was available in the aircraft, we were to take them to HMS *Devonshire*. We landed the aircraft on the pick up point and a lot of children started appearing – they were all so small! Engine power wasn't a problem, but we only had a maximum of thirteen seats. As this was an active operational area and we needed to get the children away and to safety, I filled the back of the aircraft up until I couldn't get any more

16

in then covered the door so none of the children would fall out when we took off. The ship was only five miles away, so it was only a short hop. We landed on HMS *Devonshire*, the crew lashed the Wessex to the deck and then some guys came under the rotor blades to escort the children out of the doorway and into the ship's hangar. The youngsters loved the flight, having never been in a helicopter before, and as I got them out I was counting, 1,2,3,4,5...17, 18...21, 22. I then checked just to make sure I had not lost one down the back end of the aircraft; twenty-two children rescued, not a bad result!

There were a few more evacuations from Nicosia, including one from the Russian Embassy; they were quite pleased to get out. One gave me a postcard of the Kremlin and they all signed it; a nice keepsake given that we were still involved in the Cold War.

Later there was a not-so-nice-job, and a very new experience for me. A Turkish warship was active around the north of Cyprus, about five miles out to sea. A Turkish fighter bomber came out of the thick cloud and, by mistake, attacked the ship – his own country's ship. The attack was very effective; the fighter bombed it and put a couple of rockets into it, which set the craft on fire, destroying the ship. The crew abandoned the sinking hulk and we were tasked with their recovery. Most of the survivors had been rescued, though I'm not sure by whom. The ship had caught fire and those crewmembers who had not survived had been burnt and drowned. Our task was to recover their bodies.

The only way to do that is with a sprawl net, which allows the bodies to be scooped out of the water. I remember to this day the smell of the bodies as we recovered them. Some were in one piece, some not; but we had a job to do. It's the stuff of nightmares if you can't blank it out of your mind.

On a short notice call we had to go and pick up some more refugees from near Famagusta. There was a line of old folks, men and women from the local village. We landed and the MAOT (Mobile Air Operations Team) were organising the queue to embark the older and most infirm first. Two young lads attempted to jump the queue and get on board the helicopter first. They came running along the line and tried to jump into the aircraft ahead of an old woman and child. I put my size 10 boot straight into the first guy's chest. He went down like a sack of spuds. The second guy didn't even attempt to get on board, he picked his mate up and I got the MAOT to send them to the back of the line. It was so satisfying; I'm not a violent man by any means, but standing up to bullies is a good thing – and I am sure the old folks enjoyed what they saw.

At the end of the Cyprus evacuation, we had rescued hundreds of men, women and children. Rolls Royce (RR) gave us all a Rolls Royce Rescue Tie, because we had RR engines in the Wessex; I don't remember any recognition from either the UK, Greek or Cyprus governments though.

A week later, after some more intense flying, we were on our way home, via Malta and Gibraltar. One last run ashore in Malta with the same bunch as usual, Pete Mesney, Tim Kelly, Ron Arscott, Keith 'Buck' Taylor, Charley Hope, Brian Spendlow, Kieran 'Paddy' Murry, Lou Armstrong and me. We were in a bar at a table in the corner, and right in the corner was Lou, who was a bit of a joker when he had a few beers inside him. He was also a good sprinter and gymnast. Needing a pee, Lou left the table, which was full of glasses and drinks. On his return, instead of going around the table Lou decided to do a forward somersault over the table to his chair. Of course he didn't make it, having been drinking all afternoon; he landed flat on his back on top of all the glasses. He destroyed all the glasses full of our drinks, fell to the floor, then, to our astonishment, leapt up with not one cut or bruise on him. It did cost him though – he had to refill all the drinks he had just destroyed. That was the last night out from HMS *Hermes* before returning across the Bay of Biscay again to Cath. I was glad to finally get home at long last.

Back at the squadron base in Yeovilton we carried on with more training – guided by the old adage 'train hard, fight easy'. On one of these training tasks, two of us, Vic Barker, an old and bold Petty Officer, and I were selected to do the Air Despatchers Course, where we would learn to pack and despatch loads from our aircraft by parachute. The exciting thing was, we first had to learn to do it out of the back of Hercules transport aircraft, which was a totally different affair. We started doing all the study at RAF Thorney Island in Hampshire, not far from Portsmouth. A Warrant Officer from the Air Despatch wing at Brize Norton was carrying out all the instruction. We started the practical phase the following week, after learning to pack the loads and parachutes. The loads consisted of dummy stores and light protective packing. They weighed from 500lbs up to 2,000lbs and were attached by a static line, so when you pushed them out, the parachute would hopefully self-deploy. We started on light loads, but there was a technique to getting the despatch point correct, to make the landing point. I had despatched parachutists previously and had used this technique before. The aircraft climbs to 2,000ft and then you throw out a steamer (a long piece to ribbon with a weight at one end) over the landing zone (LZ), then watch how far the streamer drifts downwind.

You mark the point where the ribbon has landed and when you despatch the parachute load or person, the same distance, but upwind from the LZ and that is your release point, to make the LZ (hopefully, if you get it right).

The despatches went quite well and we soon got the hang of the technique, getting fairly close to the LZ most times (good technique, or just lucky?)

Two days later we moved back to Yeovilton to try the technique out of the back of our Wessex Mk5s. The exercise was exactly the same, just from a different aircraft. A small cabin area and out of the door of the Wessex Mk5, compared to a huge door and ramp in the Hercules.

We repacked the loads and parachutes again, only this time we loaded them in the aircraft one at a time; the weight was too much for any more in the Wessex. I then flew down to Merrifield (Yeovilton's satellite airfield) to complete the course, with practical despatching of parachute loads from the backdoor of a helicopter. Vic decided he would drive, as he lived in Cornwall and would go on home for the weekend directly from Merrifield as soon as we had finished. He decided to park his nice newish car on the airfield, about 200 yards upwind from the LZ we had briefed.

Because we were on a parachuting exercise, the airfield was closed to other aircraft. We landed at Merrifield quite close to the LZ and picked Vic up, briefed the tower over the radio about what we intended to do, and started the exercise. I was to go first; we climbed, threw the steamer out, I decided where my release point was, checked my pack and that the parachute static line was attached correctly, all was good. At the release point, I threw the load out, which weighed 500lbs, the parachute opened. As we circled round the view was slightly different from out of the Hercules. I thought the load would miss its point, but it landed about 50 yards upwind from the LZ.

Vic was next, we landed, put his 800lb load into the aircraft, he checked the parachute and static line and we took off. Same procedure again as I had done previously, but as we came to the release point, Vic decided that because my load had landed slightly upwind, he would despatch the load early. He threw the load out and again, as we circled, he was calling where the load was going, at first his voice was calm, then the pitch started to rise slightly, then he started panicking. The wind had dropped slightly and the load, being slightly heavier, was going to land short of the LZ, about where Vic had parked his car. There was nothing we could do about it, as the 800lb load drifted closer and closer to his car. There was real panic in his voice now and with about 100ft to drop, it looked like the load would crush his car. At the last second a gust of wind blew the load to one side and it missed his car by about 20 yards. It was so close that the parachute canopy was hanging over one side of the car. It was quite funny really; at least the rest of us thought so, but I don't think Vic saw the funny side of it at all. We landed to carry on loading, but before we started again, Vic moved his car about 800 yards away, well clear of the LZ, just in case! Another lesson learnt.

We passed the course OK though, and the following week we were awarded our Air Despatchers Wings. The following weeks saw the squadron absorbed back into Yeovilton life and we were looking forward to Christmas leave.

Historically, aircrewmen had to get promotion through their original (parent) branch because at that time, rating aircrewman was an additional qualification, not a trade. This policy was changed in April 1974 when the Navy Board decided that as aircrewmen spent all their working life in aviation rather than being in their parent branch (which could have been as an electrician, chef, stoker or any other branch in the RN) a Rating Aircrewman's Branch should be established. All qualified aircrewmen were given the option to remain in their parent branch until the end of that posting/draft, or transfer to the Aircrewman's Branch, where promotion and qualifying courses would take place in the aviation role. I had been quite lazy and had done no promotional qualifications as an electrician in my parent branch, so I decided to transfer. This would give me a new opportunity in the job I preferred.

The squadron now had a pilot from the royal family on 845. Prince Charles had just joined the squadron from 707 with Red Dragon Flight (Two Wessex Mk5s specially maintained for him), he had completed his operational flying training and would now be part of the front-line commando squadron.

At the end of the year I was posted off the squadron and moved to 846 Squadron, a small unit with four Wessex Mk5 helicopters, which carried out all the trials and tests of the techniques utilised on the front-line units. It also supported the Special Forces at the time. But just before I left 845 to join my new unit, the decision was made that Leading Hand would be the lowest rank in the Aircrewman's Branch. The squadron had four Able rate aircrewmen at the time: Charley Hope, Ian (Aggie) Weston, Brum Lavery and me; we all had to go in front of the Captain to be promoted. A line of four reprobates who had got promotion through the back door. What lucky buggers we were!

CHAPTER 2

I had just scraped through flying training on BFT and OFT when I joined 845 in early 1973, but over the last two years I had gained a good deal of experience and was quite satisfied with the comment on my report that I had 'developed into a most useful, enthusiastic and professional aircrewman'; not bad for someone who would 'not make it' when he left 848 for an aircrew course at the end of 1972.

It was now the end of 1974 and I realised I had been lazy with regards to my career; I had got my Leading Hand rate by default and felt I should do something proactive for a change. Hence, I put in for the promotional exam for a place on Petty Officer Qualifying Course. After a lot of hard work and studying, I passed my exam two months later.

Chapter 3

Cath left the WRNS in the summer of 1974; if she had remained or gained promotion, she would have been drafted away from Yeovilton and we wanted to stay together in our house. She got a job in the Civil Service, as the secretary for the Chaplaincy (the priest's and padre's office), which was based at RNAS Yeovilton.

After Christmas leave I joined 846 Squadron at the beginning of 1975. I knew most of the guys flying on the squadron, it was a small unit and a great place to work. The squadron were specialists in fighter evasion and tactical flying, which would come in very handy later on in my flying career. As we were the experts in fighter evasion we had to teach the RAF, as they had not done this type of flying before. A Puma arrived from RAF Benson, we briefed the crew and went to fly. Due to its flying characteristics, the Puma did not respond like a Wessex; it was unable to flare and fast stop and stay low level (nose up to stop quickly), so we had to adapt their flying techniques by employing a roll and flare technique to carry out a fast stop and remain low level. It worked and we managed to evade the attacks from the fighters.

The year was much more settled than the previous few years, with not so much time away. A couple of trips to Denmark and Norway on trials, but most of the time at home with Cath. We settled into our routine and enjoyed the summer and time together.

The senior aircrewman on the squadron was a Fleet Chief Aircrewman (Warrant Officer 1 (WO1)) called Kentspear, everyone called him KB. He was as old as the hills and had been flying since the end of the Second World War, but he was as keen as any junior aircrewman and mad as a box of frogs. He would come up with some weird ideas. On one occasion, he wanted to fly two Wessex in formation line astern (one behind the other) and then do an inflight transfer of a person from one aircraft to the other by the winch wire – and all at 60 knots. He needed a large person for this, and selected

22

me as the idiot who would do it. I told him where to go in no uncertain terms, and he decided that maybe it was not the best idea after all.

In the summer of 1975 Cath announced that she was pregnant with our first child, which would be due in April 1976. This was great news, as we had been trying for a while to start a family.

The end of the year was approaching fast and my boss suggested that to broaden my career further, it would be a good move to do a Search and Rescue (SAR) tour. As a commando aircrewman, part of the job is to cover the SAR when you are at sea, but it is not as involved as being on a SAR flight covering civil and military incidents around the country. Without doubt a rewarding and fulfilling job. So, taking his advice, I put in for the course at Royal Naval Air station Culdrose on 771 SAR Squadron; I was accepted and was drafted there to start the SAR course at the end 1975.

The course instructor was a friend of mine, Petty Office Malcolm (Alf) Tupper, a gentleman and a scholar. Also on the course was a student called Buck Taylor, a Leading Hand SAR Diver, and Chief Petty Officer Aircrewman (CPOACMN) Bob Niblock who had been one of my instructors on 707 during my OFT. The aircraft in which we would do our course was the Wessex Mk1, a single engine aircraft that was great for SAR as you could start it and get airborne in only a few seconds, the same aircraft I had done my basic flying training in at Portland.

The course lasted six weeks and was great fun. I learnt a lot about the SAR world, improved my dead reckoning navigation techniques and skills as the aircraft had no navigation aids, much like the Wessex Mk5, plus we gained experience in all aspects of SAR. This was all while flying with a single pilot and SAR diver as a composite crew.

At the end of the course we had a land away (detachment) to Jersey as part of our final exam. There would be two aircraft and we would work with Jersey lifeboat on an SAR exercise. The social side of it was great and the people of Jersey really looked after us; they played the game on the exercise, making it as real life as possible – lots of blood and bodies. After the exercise we were all told we had passed and where we would go next. I would be drafted to 772 SAR Squadron at Portland Air Station. Things were getting better in my flying career, as on the course I achieved a first-class pass in the air and also in my ground subjects.

I joined 772 Squadron at Portland after Christmas leave 1975. Again, the people were a great bunch of guys; I knew the CPOACMN Dave Airey very well. The SAR job on the squadron was a great experience. If you brought someone back alive it was fantastic, but not so good if you brought a body back. The military sense of humour helped to cut through the sadness though.

One time we were called out to rescue a windsurfer who had got into difficulty about ten miles south of Weymouth. We scrambled, got airborne and were with him in about eight minutes. I lowered the diver to double lift the surfer up on the winch wire. When we got him safely into the helicopter, he complained that we were not able to recover his 3.5 metre board and 7 metre sail! He was suffering from hypothermia and in another couple of hours would have been in a serious way, even though he was wearing a wetsuit. We took him back to Weymouth and dropped him off at the hospital. A week later, he sent the squadron a bill for his board and sail, so we sent the cheeky bugger a bill for £4,000 for rescuing him. We heard nothing more.

Although the job was satisfying, I had a slight clash of personalities with my divisional officer; I had flown with him on 845 two years before (we had history). He was an arrogant young lieutenant pilot, who I had never really got on with. Later, just after Easter leave 1976, a job opportunity came up on a recruiting flight, working out of 707 NACS at Yeovilton. I put in for it and got it. I was heading back to Yeovilton again and as I was still living at home in Bower Hinton, it also meant an end to the hour-long commute to and from work each day.

The recruiting flight crew was formed at the end of April. We had one Wessex Mk5 (call sign PT, which then became RN), one pilot, one crewman and about eight engineers. We were tasked with going around the country, attending shows and schools, recruiting for the Royal Navy and Royal Marines. I had done my abseil instructor course and attached to the flight were two Royal Marines who, as part of the display, would abseil 200ft into an arena. Attached to us also was the Royal Marine freefall parachute team. We worked up for two weeks before we were ready to go on the road. The only problem was that Cath was due to have our baby in late April, but she was two weeks late. She gave birth to Kieran, our first son, on 2 May; it was a fantastic experience watching our child being born, but the flight was due to leave the next day. There was no one else to do the job, so I had to go. Cath's mother came down to help, but it's not the same as having your husband there.

The flight went on the road and the routine for the show was that the pilot, Grahame Fowler, and I would do an aerial display, a few wing overs, fast stops, tight turns and climbs, then come in and start to winch. One of the engineers would be dressed as an old woman being chased by a policeman. As the policeman got hold of the woman I would winch her clear. Then a terrorist attack would take place; I would abseil the two Royal Marines in and the rest of the crew would have a gun fight. The crowd loved it. Then we would get the freefall team in, climb to 10,000ft and throw them out to land on the LZ in the centre of the showground. The show went around the country, Liverpool, Sheffield, Bridlington, Birmingham, Nottingham, London, Edinburgh and Brighton, plus lots of other small places where the RN/RM had never been before.

Everything was going OK until we went to Brighton. We did our display in the grounds of Brighton and Hove Albion football club. The wind was gusting, but the jump leader of the freefall team said it was OK to jump. I had eight parachutists in the back, they all prepared to jump and on the count three they left the aircraft. I watched them down, counted the chutes as I normally did, 6, 7, 8 chutes. All good.

The wind then got up a bit more and the ground crew called to inform us, but the team had already jumped. As they approached overhead the stadium and the LZ, the wind became gustier. Two landed short of the ground, three long and two managed to get into the ground, with one still to land. He was the RSM, the jumpmaster and also the lightest, so had more air time than the others. He was approaching the ground and would have made it OK, but just as he approached the centre of the ground and descended below the main grandstand, he lost all his lift and plummeted to the ground from about 80ft, there was nothing he could do to stop it. Unfortunately, he sustained serious injuries to his neck and back. The medics were really good, but all they could do was put him on a board. We landed in the ground and took him straight to Stoke Mandeville Hospital. He lived, but was paralysed from the neck down and I believe he never walked again.

A month after the accident with the RSM of the freefall team, the whole flight was up at Whitby, North Yorks. We were working out of Butlin's in Filey, but the aircraft was positioned at Bridlington airfield nearby. The freefall team were also doing some training with the company that provided their parachutes, a firm called Irvine. The Irvine team were doing a series of jumps and we got permission from the RN for them to jump out of our aircraft. A few days later, the company offered to take Graham and I up and let us jump, provided we had the correct training. Stan, one of the Marines gave us the training and so we were ready to go. I had never jumped before (as aircrew what's the sense of jumping out of a serviceable aircraft!). We were to jump out of a Cessna 185, an over the wing aircraft. Because of my size and weight, about 16 stone at the time, I was to go first because I needed an extra-large canopy. We took off and did the streamer drop and then climbed to 3,000ft, the nerves were starting now. The door was opened and I was ushered to the entrance. By now I was thinking, 'what am I doing here?' Then Stan, who was also the jumpmaster, asked if I was OK. What else could I say. I was sitting on the edge of the door with 3,000ft of nothing below me. All of a sudden, he said 'Go for it', so I did, without thinking. It was a static line jump, so as I left the aircraft, I made to get into the stable position, with my arms and legs out at 45 degrees. I shouted, '1001, 1002, 1003 Check'. I looked up and saw that my canopy was deploying (thank God). It was then that I began to enjoy the jump; I had dropped 500ft before the canopy had deployed fully, so I had 2,500ft to float down. It was great, no sense of falling at all. I steered using the guide lines attached to the canopy, but then all of a sudden, I could see the Drop Zone. I had heard of ground rush before, but the experience was worse. All of a sudden, I was rushing to the ground and because we were using round parachutes, you can't really steer into wind like a modern para-wing chute. Then I hit the ground, luckily the training worked and I para-rolled from my side to back with my legs slightly up. I managed to bang my head slightly, but I was wearing a helmet. I had missed the DZ only by about 15 yards, which was pretty good for a first attempt. After the first jump I volunteered to do another two and the more confident I got, the more I enjoyed it. There are some things you need to tick off your bucket list and this was one of them.

While at Butlin's, we used to go for a few drinks with the flight crew and the Royal Marine freefall team. After one fairly late night we went to a café for something to eat, I got a burger then went to bed. The next morning six of us were called in to see the RSM. He accused us of mooning to a woman in the café. We denied it, but one lad was a bit shy about the incident. The next thing we knew, we were having an identity parade outside the café. The woman was in the café and we were all facing out from the window, she picked out one of the young Marines – how she recognised him I will never know, it was dark outside the night before and he was now fully clothed; we just thought she wanted to get to know him a little better, but who knows. He got three days punishment and had to apologise to the lady, what happened after I don't know.

The summer of 1976 was so hot and everyone thought it would never come to an end, it just went on and on. No rain at all. The grass had gone brown and there were hosepipe bans all over the country. Cath told me that Kieran was grumpy in the heat; wearing nothing other than a nappy in his cot, but still roasting hot and unable to sleep. He cried a lot and Cath was finding it difficult to cope without any help. I felt so sorry for her, but there was nothing I could do to help from afar.

The rest of the summer went fine. I managed to get home to Yeovilton about five times over the five months while we were on the road, which wasn't a lot given that Kieran had grown some every time I saw him. Cath managed well while I was away, all things considered. As some people say: 'that's the life of a military wife'; it's great when the husbands are at home, but they spend so much time away that the wives have to be quite independent and confident in living on their own for long periods. Cath was very good at that; she didn't like it, but she was very good at it.

One of our final displays took place in Nottingham, the aircraft was being parked at Hucknall Airfield just on the northern boundary of the city. We were living in a pub next door to the main train station, the Bentinck Hotel as I recall, it is now a Starbucks.

All had been going well during our second display at Nottingham air show. The display had been carried out without incident, we landed, embarked the freefall team on board and climbed to 10,000ft where we held in an orbit at altitude while the Pitts Specials (small bi-planes) carried out their display. After about two minutes in the holding pattern, there was a bang and smoke started issuing from the starboard (right-hand) engine. The engine had failed in a big way. The remaining engine was fine, but we needed to land. The freefall team were just about to jump out, because they thought it safer to jump and get out as quickly as possible. With the main door open, I stood in front of them and stopped them. They did not realise that the Pitts Specials team were right under us and had they jumped they may have collided with the two small aircraft. They were not happy lads! Consequently, we called air traffic and declared a PAN: an emergency which is not catastrophic at the time, but could develop into a major incident if the aircraft did not land as soon as possible. We were cleared to land, but had to go to the north, back to Hucknall. To keep the aircraft in a safe configuration, we carried out a running landing and touched down safely, the engineers had to change the engine, which they did in remarkable time and we were displaying again the next day.

My mother and father were living in Nottingham at the time and I had not seen them for ages, so I made the effort to go and visit them. I told them that we were going out that night, and to mend a few bridges given I hadn't seen them for so long, I asked them to come along. Not wanting to miss out on a few beers, they said yes. We met them later in the centre of town and after a few pints we ended up in a pub called the 'Trip to Jerusalem', reputedly one of the oldest inns in Britain, and situated at the base of the castle mound. After a few more drinks in there, my mother and father were getting very tipsy. Then my mother started singing – as was her want! The landlord said he had no licence for music and that she should stop singing; my mother politely told him where to go and carried on. At that the landlord told us to get out, and barred us from the pub. That's some claim to fame, being barred from the Trip to Jerusalem because of my mother's antics!

The flight eventually came back to Yeovilton at the end of August and we took some deserved leave. It was nice to have some time with Cath and Kieran at last. Kieran was now nearly five months old and I had hardly seen him; it was time to catch up.

On returning to 707 Squadron, which was the training unit at the time, I was given a minor instruction role with the junior course. The flying was good. Lots of very low-level around Dartmoor and Exmoor. Then on 28 September, a call came in that there had been an accident in the North Sea off of the coast of Holland, about 100 miles north of Den Helder. Two of our ships, a minesweeper (HMS *Fittleton*) and a frigate (HMS *Mermaid*) had been doing some cross-decking with a light jackstay (a line from one ship to the other, to pass people or stores across).

Something went wrong while they were doing this; apparently the minesweeper's bow went under the frigate's bow. The next instant the minesweeper rolled over and turned turtle. Most of the crew managed to abandon ship, but twelve didn't manage to get out. Of the twelve who died, eleven were reservists and one was a regular serving sailor, he was a stoker called Gerry Hoey.

We were tasked with supporting the ships recovering the bodies and the ships around the recovery in the North Sea. Two hours later, we got airborne to a Dutch Navy airfield called De Kooy, on the north coast of Holland. The weather en route was awful. Low cloud, rain and wind. That's when one's navigation skills really come into play, especially over 100 miles of sea with no navigation aids to help.

We landed at De Kooy in the dark and got our briefings. The main task was to repatriate the bodies, from HMS *Achilles* and HMS *Jaguar* which were the ships on site, by the *Fittleton*. After a few days most of the bodies had been recovered from the overturned ship. Not a task that anyone really wants to undertake.

My next flight out was to HMS *Jaguar*, a Leopard Class frigate which was coordinating the recovery mission, to deliver stores and mail to the

CHAPTER 3

ship. The weather was really bad, low cloud, base about 500ft and the visibility was about 1,500 metres. We had an extra drop-tank of fuel to give the aircraft an extended endurance, giving us about three-and-a-half hours in the air. I got a position for the ship as we took off, it was 110 miles away in the North Sea. Our aircraft had a UHF direction finder, which told us if the transmission from a radio was to the left or right of us; unfortunately, we had no radio contact with the ship.

The Wessex normally flew at 90 knots, so it would take us about one hour to cover 110 statute miles. As we got within ten miles of the rendezvous point according to my calculations, we still had no radio contact. I was assessing the wind from the surface and changing my navigation plan constantly. With four minutes to go there was still no contact. The weather had become increasingly worse, cloud base now at 400ft and visibility about 500 metres. We were flying at 350ft above sea level.

I decided to start a search plan because dead-reckoning navigation is not an exact science. I calculated a plan known as an expanding square search. This is used in the SAR role for searching an area from a central point expanding out to cover all options and directions. With two minutes to run, the plan was set. I briefed the senior pilot, Dave Wiggery, who was flying the Wessex and said, 'In two minutes, we will start a square search, the first heading will be 350 degrees for one minute, then the next heading after that will be 085 degrees.' With 20 seconds to go, I said, 'Standby to turn, next heading 350 turn, NOW, NOW—'

'There it is, I don't believe it!' Dave said, before I had chance to say the third 'NOW'. He was astonished. We had approached the *Jaguar*, along the port stern quarter. He couldn't believe what we had done, and frankly neither could I; 110 miles with no navigation aids and we came along side on time, in the correct position and all done in appalling weather. A bit of luck came in to play perhaps, but all the same it was a job well done. My training, hard work and experience had definitely paid off this time and the pilot complimented me after the sortie for my performance.

It took till 5 October to recover all the bodies and equipment, it was only on completion that we could recover our aircraft and crews back to Yeovilton, which happened on 6 October, yet another detachment completed.

Events carried on at pace on 707 with flying and ground instruction, but life was pretty good. This was military life though and you don't normally get to stay in one place for too long, at least that never seemed to happen to me! November came and I got the dreaded phone call from Charlie Wines. He was the Lieutenant Commander in charge of the aircrewman drafting and appointments. He had been around in the Second World War as a (TAG) Telegraphist Air Gunner and was getting on a bit long in the tooth. He played drafting in his own style (if you scratch my back, I'll scratch yours). Well the recruiting job was a bit of a bonus, but now he needed someone to go front line on to 845 Squadron. He had already spoken to my boss, so it was all done and dusted before I even got the phone call.

At the beginning of December 1976 I was on the move, back to 845 again. I emptied my locker and packed all my flying clothing plus my desert and Arctic kit into a couple of kit bags with my normal naval uniform for temperate conditions and whites for the tropics. There seemed to be so much kit, I wasn't sure where it all came from. Going back to 845 was like going back to an old mate's place. The office block had changed, but the routine was still much the same. A lot of the people had, like me, left the squadron and then returned again, so I knew many of them from 707, 846, 848 or 845 Squadron. I settled in to 845 during December, then after Christmas it was back to Norway, first in Bardufoss, then back onboard *Hermes* again.

The Fleet Air Arm was in transition at the time, with the large fixed-wing carriers being scrapped and new through-deck cruisers being built. These were smaller than ships such as HMS *Ark Royal*, *Eagle* and *Hermes*, which had flown Phantoms, Buccaneers, Sea Vixens and Gannets from their decks. We had lost all our big fixed-wing aircraft and the Navy thought that the way ahead was the Sea Harrier, a sea version of the ground attack Harrier that the RAF had flown for a few years. So it was that the deck on HMS *Hermes* was converted to accept the Sea Harrier. It had a ramp built on the forward part of the flight deck, to allow the Harrier to take off with more payload. As in all military weapons systems though, they have to be tested before we can operate them.

The next two weeks were spent doing plane guard for the Harrier trials, we had to be ready each time the Harriers operated from the deck. The helicopter crew consisted of one pilot, a crewman and an SAR diver. If the Harrier crashed into the sea, the diver would jump from the helicopter, dive down and rescue the pilot. A technique employed for years on all the old fixed-wing carriers. Fortunately though, the trials went really well and not long after, the first deployment of the Sea Harriers went to sea on HMS *Invincible*, the first of the through deck cruisers.

After the Harrier trials we returned to Norway to carry out the normal winter exercises with the Royal Marines, just south of Tromso in northern Norway. I was now more experienced with more confidence in myself and my ability as an aircrewman and aviator. Having taken and passed my promotion exam not long after I got my advancement to Leading Hand in 1974, the next step was to complete the Petty Officer Aircrewman's Qualifying Course. The course was held at the newly commissioned Aircrewman's School at Culdrose in Cornwall. Three courses were held each year and they lasted for ten weeks. I was to attend No.10 POACMN Qualifying Course to start in the first week of May 1977.

There were seven of us on the course; Brad, Clive, Scouse, Arthur, Bomber, Fitz and myself; we were all Leading Hands. The officer in charge was a Lieutenant Observer called George Spence (nice guy), the Chief was Ken Morris, who had been my Chief on 845 in 1973, the PO instructor was initially Tony Gerrard and he was then relieved halfway through the course by PO Dave 'Polly' Parrott. The course consisted of academic and ground-based navigation type work, but in the air it was based around navigation skills, winching, load lifting, radio and crew command skills and crew resource management. Quite a difficult course. Four of the students had come from the commando and SAR roles, so the navigation skills came as second nature. The winching and load lifting were also part of our core skills. Unfortunately, the guys who had come from the Anti-Submarine Warfare roles had a bit of a struggle to keep up, because they didn't use their navigation skills while ASW flying.

In the evenings Clive and I helped Fitz, as he was struggling the most. We would give him tips and work on his dead reckoning navigation skills and his paperwork. The thing we could not help him with too much was his low-flying navigation. This is where you talk the pilot around a route, he is told what to look out for (as the crewman is looking backwards and sideways out of the helicopter doorway), then says if he can see it or not. The crewman then tells him where he should go and the whole navigation route is covered using the same techniques. For a start, you need to be able to read a map, know all the symbols and be able to describe them to the pilot who is flying the helicopter and in words he can relate to. For instance: 'Looking in your two o'clock, can you see a large valley heading off about 270 degrees, the valley has a wood on the right-hand side.' The pilot would look and confirm he has seen it. The crewman would then reply: 'We need to fly down that valley, for two miles, where it will fork; we need to take the left fork heading about 230 degrees.' This is called 'Bat and Ball' (the aircrewman would give navigational information to the pilot (bat) and the pilot would respond (ball)) and this system would get you round the route hopefully. Sometimes features are not obvious though, like disused railways and roads that are quite small, or lots of woods or lakes that are scattered all around.

On one particular trip, we all had to do two legs of low-flying navigation; I had Polly in the back with me, Brad and Fitz. Brad had started off and done his legs, then Fitz was to take over; he knew where he was, but not quite sure where he was going. We neared Bodmin Road Railway Station, just north of Liskeard in Cornwall, near the county boundary. The aircraft was heading north and the route then took us east towards Oakhampton. Fitz was following the road north, then he wanted to follow a disused railway line. Alarm bells started to ring in my head, as I was following his navigation plan. I tried to get his attention, without letting Polly see me, but Fitz was too intent on looking at the map and not outside the aircraft, or in the cabin at me. He told the pilot to follow the disused railway line, but the pilot couldn't see one. Fitz then started getting agitated with the pilot and asked what he could see and what heading he was on. The pilot explained what he could see, but Fitz was confused, as the aircraft was now going the wrong way. I had to help him! I got my map out and tried to point out where we were and explain to him that he needed the pilot to follow his commands and that the disused railway line that Fitz was telling the pilot to follow was actually the county boundary, the symbols are very much alike, but not the same size or pattern. It can be quite confusing for someone who is not used to doing navigation at low level and in a high-energy environment. Anyway, eventually we got to where we were going and at the end of the day we all passed the sortie.

The course continued, the tasks got harder, the navigation more precise and the ground school got much more demanding. Part of the course was to do Morse code, which we had done before during our flying careers, but not on a regular basis. On this course they expected the students to do eight words a minute; that's not too hard using sound, but this was eight words a minute using light, with an Aldiss flashing lamp. I must admit, I struggled with that more than any other part of the course.

My course nearly came to an end one night ashore in Helston, though. We were in the Beehive pub having a few drinks and the circus was in town. I was standing on some small steps up to the bar when a lad had pushed by me twice, and on his return he barged me out of the way. Before I could say anything, I had four guys punching me; I wheeled round and started going for anything that moved, but was outnumbered. I was kicking and biting, and then I felt this chair crashing on my back. I went down and at that point the owner stepped in and got in the way. I thought: this is the time to go, no heroics here! I had survived, but only just. I did wonder where my mates had got to.

CHAPTER 3

The next morning I had a black eye, a bashed nose and a big fat lip. I didn't think I had come off too badly, but when I went to work and the instruction staff saw me, I thought it was the end of the course for me. It was a struggle to get my flying helmet on, but I managed. I was going to complete this course, no matter what. When I got home at the weekend and Cath saw me, she said, 'You've been fighting again.' I said, 'what do you mean again? It's a long time since I was ever in a fight.' But she was right, I was getting too old for this sort of thing.

At the end of the POACMN Qualifying Course, we all had to do a final Air Test, involving navigation and secondary roles, like winching and loads. We all passed thank God! Next came the ground tests. These were more difficult I thought, but again we all passed. The results came out on the last morning of our course. Three of us had got first-class passes in the air and on the ground, even Fitz got a good pass in the air, so he had pulled his socks up over the second-half of the course.

You always have rivalry between students, don't you? No exception here. Clive Brookes and I had been nip and tuck throughout the course. The ground results came out and I had beaten Clive by about 2 per cent, and that was down to his recognition test. On the flying side, he had got a six assessment, which is pretty damn good, but I had a seven. I had come top, which was great for my confidence. We had passed the course and were all now qualified for promotion to Petty Officer, however promotion was also dependent on your write up and the assessment given from your squadron Commanding Officer, so the better the write up the more likely you were to get quick advancement.

Along with this, Clive and I, having done so well on the course, were offered a change of role as a crewman. We were given the chance to become fixed-wing crewmen, known as communication crewmen, flying in Herons and Devons. These were four and two engine passenger aircraft and the crewman did all the navigation and radio, through airways and at altitude. A great job, but my squadron had just been told that we would be starting to operate in Northern Ireland and I fancied the tactical operations over the water. Both Clive and I turned down the offer. I knew I might regret it in the future, but I had made my choice. The final run ashore was on the last night of our course, it was a great party at Brad's house, all the students and instructors attended and gave us a chance to let our hair down (I still had some then) and have a few drinks; the next day, it was home to Cath and Kieran.

The course had finished at the end of June. I managed to take some leave and then it was back to the squadron at Yeovilton. After a quick flight

33

check, we were back to normal flying duties. The next detachment away was on *Hermes* again, up to Scotland and working out of a small airstrip called Plockton, which wasn't far from Oban on the west coast. We had been ashore for about two days working with 45 Commando, when all the aircraft were told to return to Plockton. We landed and were told that something was going down and the aircraft had to get back to Yeovilton, with all the squadron kit, ASAP. The ship had already left, to go around to Edinburgh, so could not be used. The plan was to fly back overnight to Yeovilton. The time was now dragging on and dusk was about two hours away. All the crews manned their aircraft, all the kit we could take was put in and we set off to Prestwick airport, south of Glasgow. It was a two-hour round trip back to Plockton and we would each have to do two trips to take all the ground machinery, equipment and personnel down to Prestwick. We weren't sure what would happen then – stay overnight at Prestwick or head south?

The big government and military machine works when it wants to, it kicks in and becomes a slick and effective organisation. The second time we landed at Prestwick, two Hercules air transport aircraft were waiting to ferry all our kit and ground crews to Yeovilton. There were twelve Wessex, in two formations of six. We refuelled again at Prestwick and then set off for Yeovilton. The plan was to fly over the Irish Sea down to RAF Valley on Anglesey and refuel again. We had operated many times from there and I thought it would take ages to refuel twelve aircraft in the dead of night, but on arrival at about 2am the aircraft landed, taxied to a line of six refuel spots and to our astonishment, six fuel bowsers rolled up and refuelled us all at once. We vacated the spots, then the other six Wessex got refuelled and left shortly after. The system really does work, when needed!

The flight down to Yeovilton was pretty straightforward. We landed at about 5am, put the aircraft in the hangar, then the whole squadron were briefed and told why we had come back in such a rush. The government, had been informed that an incident had taken place in Belize, a British enclave in South America. The squadron was to stand-by, in case the incident escalated into something worse. It was the first time I had ever flown through the night; we had taken off in daylight and landed after dawn the next day. All the crews were exhausted, so the boss said go home and sleep, but to keep in touch. At 6am I knocked on the front door and Cath was shocked to see me; it was the first time I had ever come home early from a detachment, I was normally at least a day late. Nothing ever materialised in Belize and three days later we were stood down, to carry on as normal.

CHAPTER 3

Cath and I had been trying for a second child for a while and at the end of September she told me she was pregnant again. Our second baby was due in May of the next year, 1978. Hopefully, I would be around this time to help look after the baby – with any luck that is. But watch this space, it's never that simple.

During the next few weeks the planning went ahead for a minor exercise around the north cape of Scotland and the Shetlands based on board HMS *Fearless*. The exercise was going well, the weather was cold but clear. The flying was OK, lots of troop moves and load lifting. Late one evening I was flying with Lieutenant Bill Sample and Sub-Lieutenant Norman Lees, we had dropped ten Royal Marines off on the West Coast of the Shetlands and were transiting back to the east coast, which took us over the spine of the islands. It was night now and very dark and we were at about 2,000ft. As we approached the highest point of the ridge line, Norman, who was flying the aircraft from the right-hand seat, said he saw a light to the north out of the left window. Bill looked left and they were talking about this light. I was in the doorway and all of a sudden, I saw a flash from our anti-collision light which reflected on the surface of the ridge! I bellowed 'UP, UP, UP!' Norman pulled the collective lever up and we shot up to height again. While the two pilots had been looking out of the left window, they had let the collective lever drop and we were slowly descending. The only reason we didn't crash into the ridgeline was that I saw the reflection of the anti-collision light on the surface of the ridgeline; the aircraft was at about 20ft above the ground when we started to recover. Another close call! How many cat's lives gone?

After returning from Scotland we started the work-up to go to Northern Ireland (NI). We watched the news from the province with great interest now. Although we had always taken note of what was going on there, now I was going to be part of it. The flying consisted of lots of ultra-low-level flying, finding points in the corners of fields, landing in confined areas and landing not more than 15 yards away from a selected 8-figure grid reference. The troops don't need to be humping all their kit and weapons any further than necessary. Of course, in those days there was no GPS system and the Wessex Mk5 had no navigation aids to help with finding an accurate grid reference. Everything was carried out manually, so we had to be on top of the navigation at all times.

After all the training and operational flying exercises, we still needed to do all our ground training, weapons training, first aid training and all of the intelligence briefings.

Eventually it was time to go across the water to NI, I said my farewells to Cath and Kieran. I think Cath was a little worried. The news from NI had not been good, lots of bombings and terrorist attacks, especially against the military and RUC (police). I tried to calm her, but I don't think it worked. Our tours over the water were for six weeks, so not too long. Unlike the troops, who did six-month tours.

The RAF had been out at Aldergrove for quite some time supporting the troops in the province, and we were to join them at Aldergrove and operate alongside them.

We finally got to Aldergrove during the last week of October 1977. Having completed all the familiarisation briefs and flights, we started to operate in the province and it was good to go out and do all the tasking we had trained for over the previous couple of months. The flying over the next few weeks was great, some low-level and then we might get called at short notice to do something completely different. One shout was towards Enniskillen. In the hills near the border with Southern Ireland there are a range of small hills and embedded in the hills are a series of potholes. The weather was awful, rain, low cloud and high winds. We got a call to take a rescue team to the area because five cavers were trapped in a low pothole; the water was rising due to the heavy rain and they had no air left in their tanks.

Having picked up the guys from Belfast, with all their diving gear, we devised a plan of attack. The plan was to fly south of Lough Neagh along the low ground and then west towards Enniskillen. The visibility was getting worse and worse and we were getting lower and lower, but we were still OK and so pressed on. We had a radio call just as we passed Lurgan; the rain had got worse and the flooded cave would soon be inaccessible. We needed to get there pretty quickly or the rescue could not take place, which meant the potholers would almost certainly die. The cloud got lower and the visibility reduced even further, by this stage we were following the roads and valleys that headed west. These had wires across them and we were now down to a hover taxi doing about 30 knots and going under some of the wires. The pilots had eyes out of the cockpit and I was doing the navigation, calling all the wires, turns and timings. We knew we had to get these guys to the rescue point, but that was on the side of a hill in cloud. Eventually we got to the bottom of the hill. Next, we slowly climbed the high ground and into the valley, going from one tree or road to another, until at last we made the drop off point, then we got the team out, with all their diving and rescue gear.

Our job was done but it was a close call. After grovelling around in the weeds, we decided that on the way back it would be best to climb up and get a radar service back to Aldergrove, we did that and were back at our base in forty minutes. The next day the rescue team phoned to tell us they had had only minutes to spare when they got to the five trapped guys and that without our help, the cavers would have died in the lower compartments of the potholes. Looking back, that was a job well done.

The routine tasking carried on; every sixth day we would go down to Bessbrook, which was in South Armagh. The crews would fly out of there for a 24-hour period then back to Aldergrove. South Armagh was known as the 'badlands', out of which the IRA worked. Everything went by air to the outposts like Fork Hill or Crossmaglen, all these outposts were situated on the border with Southern Ireland. The border at the time was just a road across into the south, but marked with a white cross to separate the north and south, so anyone could just drive over at any time, which made it quite easy for the 'bad guys' to come and go when they wanted. It wasn't all work of course, we had a few runs ashore. The lads were allowed out in pairs, but only to certain, so-called safe areas. At the time we had to take a weapon with us, just in case, but fortunately nothing ever happened to us. I know some others who strayed to the wrong areas and had to be helped out by the boys in green; naughty boys!

One thing in our spare time though was boredom. You either did some training or education courses, or went to the bar. Most people did the latter, but to try and keep out of the bar for as long as possible, Charlie Hope and I played squash in the evening. We would play for about two hours, take a shower, then hit the bar. At least keeping fit and playing squash kept me sane and cut the hours in the bar down a little bit. The squash was great though, and I still play even now.

The work continued at pace and after six weeks it was time to go home. We had worked quite hard and I had managed to clock up 100 flying hours on my first tour. My last flight of that first detachment to NI was down to Omagh, working with a section of troops from the resident regiment; the brief was to do Vehicle Check Points (VCPs). The routine was to have eight troops in the aircraft, land at one end of a road, drop off four soldiers, take off and then drop off the other four at the opposite end of the road. Any cars that came along would be checked at either end of the road. We would then fly round and look for anyone who had stopped or looked suspicious, and had run or reversed away from the VCP. After about four moves to set up various VCPs between Armagh and Omagh, we told the troops we had half-an-hour on task, then it was back to their landing site in Omagh. We landed the first four troops again next to a layby, which had a Morris 1100 parked in it; we thought nothing of it. Next, we landed the other four troops about one mile away down the road. After ten minutes no cars had appeared, so we called to troops on our FM Radio to run in and pick up the first four soldiers; a call came back: 'Do not land at this LZ, land 500 metres away and wait for information.' So we landed in a field 500 metres away. The Commander of the troops came in and said that the Morris 1100 was a bit dodgy and smelt of marzipan – a sure sign of explosives at the time. We were told to go back to Omagh barracks and get the sniffer dogs and bomb disposal trolley. On landing, we refuelled and got the dogs and trolley on board. Arriving back with troops again we dropped off the dogs and trolley and then had to leave to go back to Aldergrove. Another aircraft would come out later.

On our return to Aldergrove, we were met by the operations officer, who had received a call from Omagh, the Morris 1100 was all wired up and had 500lbs of explosives in the boot. Fortunately for us, the terrorists were not around to set the bomb off when we had landed, otherwise it would have been curtains. At that stage of the troubles in NI, one of the main objectives of the IRA was to destroy a helicopter; if they had been around at the time, they would have achieved their goal.

I got home later that day, 8 December, but didn't mention to Cath what had happened. I was due to go back to Aldergrove a few months later and it would have played on her mind every time I had deploy over the water.

Back on 845 squadron at Yeovilton, we had to prepare for the next trip away, which was back to Norway in the January for another winter deployment to Bardufoss. This covered all the winter training and then the exercise, which was called CLOCKWORK. But before requalifying again for Arctic conditions we had to go to the standard winter lectures and kit issue, to ensure we were prepared to operate in the snow and cold of the Norwegian winter. Just after one of the lessons we broke for stand easy (tea break) and the officer in charge told Brad Bradbury and me to go to the HQ building, where the Captain had his office. We were told that Brad and I were going to be the first to get our General Service Medal, awarded for service in Northern Ireland. In those days no one had any medals other than the Long Service Medal, or if they were old enough, medals from Borneo or the Second World War. It was great to get a gong at last, but it certainly was not going to be my last.

Chapter 4

At the start of 1978 we went to Bardufoss for our winter deployment, four aircraft to begin with, increasing to twelve for the exercises in both Northern and Southern Norway. We worked mainly with 45 Commando, the Arctic specialists in the Royal Marine Commando group and 42 Commando, who operated in the south of Norway. To keep fit I still did lots of cross-country skiing, luckily the Norwegians had built a langlauf track near Bardufoss and as it was lit, it was excellent for night skiing.

The training went well and the exercises started – that's also when the fun started, living out in the field either under canvas or, if you were unlucky, a snow hole. Lots of flying in all sorts of conditions, character-building stuff!

Part of the exercise was to deploy the Mountain and Arctic Warfare Cadre (M&AW Cadre) the specialist warfare Arctic troops for the Royal Marines. We had to insert a two-man Observation Post (OP) on top of an 8,000ft mountain, in the middle of nowhere. The approach was up the mountain and then we had to creep over the top to avoid being seen by the enemy, drop the men and their kit off, then back off and creep back down the slope without being seen. That we did; the weather was clear and cold about -15°C. The men would be up there for two days with enough water and supplies for three, we would pick them up forty-eight hours later. That was the plan anyway. When the time came, the weather had changed completely, a snowstorm with high winds had arrived, so the extraction of the M&AW troops was put back twenty-four hours. The next day the weather had not changed, we could still talk to the men and they were OK, but food was running short and it was damn cold up there, it had fallen to -30°C with the wind chill. It was decided that we could not go again until the next day. Dawn came and the weather had improved slightly; it was still snowing, but the wind had dropped to probably about 15 to 20 knots at ground level, however the OP said at their location it was about 30 knots, with poor visibility. They needed extraction as they had no water, fuel or food left and they were beginning to suffer.

The crew as a whole decided we should try and get them down, because if we didn't, there was a possibility they could die up there. The brief took place and we set off; the plan was to go along the same route as before, but approach from the other direction, as that was into wind and there was now no need for a tactical approach – it had turned into a SAR mission, life or death in this case.

The visibility was appalling, about 1,500 metres at the bottom, but as we climbed, it came down to a few metres. The technique for this style of approach is to keep visual with the ground and at least two points of reference, this allows the pilot to maintain his orientation with the wider world; combining this with the instruments means you know which way is level, up and down. I was in the back of the aircraft maintaining separation from the rocks and outcrops on the mountain and we hover-climbed up the side of the mountain at about 50ft per minute, which is pretty slow, but safer than rushing. Not that this was particularly safe at all; if anything went wrong, a rotor tip strike, falling rock, or the pilot putting in a wrong control movement, we would all die as a crew, but this was our job!

After about forty minutes we had climbed to 7,800ft and not much more to go. The visibility had improved to about 100 metres with the winds blowing the snow along, but the turbulence at the top was quite strong and was throwing the aircraft around. The pilot did a good job of handling the situation and as we approached the LZ (if you can call it that, a 5 x 5 metre piece of rock that we could only put one wheel on) the two Marines called us, saying they could hear the aircraft below them. With 50ft to go to the top of the mountain they came into view, I talked the aircraft into position and with the right wheel on the LZ (rock) and the tail hanging over a very long drop, I pulled the two men in. As they got in, one dropped an empty 5-gallon jerry can, it slid under the aircraft and I presume eventually tumbled all the way down to the next ridge line about 5,000ft below us.

We had got the troops in, but now had to get down; we couldn't climb and do a radar recovery, because ice would build on the blades and we would crash. The only way down was the reverse of the way we had come up. It took another fifty minutes to get down and when we landed we were all extremely cold and near exhaustion, it had been the most tiring mission I had ever been on, but we had brought the two Marines down alive, and everyone understood what we had done to save them. The weather eventually cleared three days later and I am positive they wouldn't have survived a long stay on top of that mountain.

CHAPTER 4

A week later we had to go to Tromso, towards the north of Norway, it was a VIP task to take a visiting team of Russians to inspect our forces South of Tromso. This was a regular deal, we did the same thing to the Russians, so no one could say the British or Soviet military were doing anything illegal under a treaty which had been signed a few years before.

The trip up to Tromso went without hitch. We landed on the taxi pad, the snow had been cleared, which left sheet ice to park the aircraft on. This was normal for us and we had some chocks with spikes on to put under the wheels and stop the helicopter from sliding around. The Russians were the typical KGB and high-ranking Soviet generals. There was one KGB officer who reminded me of Herr Flick from the TV comedy *Allo! Allo!*; he wore a long leather coat, a wide brimmed hat and carried a cane. He would not listen to any part of the safety brief or warning I gave him about flying (arrogant bugger, I thought). When we landed I put the chocks in, the rotors were still turning and I waited by the door to let them step down on to the hard standing, or ice standing as it was. The Herr Flick lookalike started to climb out via the step, I put my hand out to help him, but he discarded it with disdain and as he put his foot to the ice, he went arse over tit. It was like something out of a Charlie Chaplin movie. I tried to keep a straight face, but he must have seen me laugh, I wish I'd had a movie camera at the time. The generals and officers who got out next took more care, but they did have a wry smile on their faces. I am sure they thought, like me, that it was hilarious.

When the winter exercise finally finished, the flight made its way back to Yeovilton but this time, rather than coming back by sea, we flew back. Down to Bergen, across the North Sea, fuelling on an oil rig and then to Aberdeen for the night. Next day down to RAF Woodvale in Lancashire and finally to Yeovilton. It was now the beginning of April, Easter leave would happen next, then back over the water to NI again in June.

Our second child was due around 11 May and I was programmed to leave and go back to Aldergrove at the beginning of June. The pregnancy went fine, the 11th came and went. Ten days had gone by when the midwife said if the baby didn't come in the next four days, Cath would be induced. On the morning of the 25th, Cath was induced, her mother had come down to help and look after Kieran and later that day we had another little baby boy. We named him Simon. It was good having Cath's mum down to help, as I was leaving two weeks later and would not be around to help, but this time at least it was only for six weeks, not six months. A proper little family now: parents, two children, house and car; all was looking good.

That year passed quite quickly, Kieran was now 2½, Simon 6 months old – and this baby slept. I did two more tours in NI, with lots of good flying, most of it in South Armagh. Lots of jobs around the border into Crossmaglen and Fork Hill. One night we had to go looking for two RUC police officers who had gone out in a Land Rover; we searched long and hard but could not find them. Unfortunately, the next morning we had a call to go out and recover their bodies. Everyone suspected the IRA of ambushing the poor guys. They must have put about 200 rounds into the side of the vehicle. The bodies – or what was left of them – were laid out on the road in body bags. What a waste of life I thought, why do people do such things to others? The rest of the day was a bit sombre. Two weeks later I was home again after another tour and back into normal tasking on the mainland.

Another tour in Aldergrove came after Christmas, then came a call from Charlie Wines, the drafter. He wanted me to move, but this time it was in my favour! I would be drafted back to 707 Squadron around Easter of 1979, that's where I had completed my operational training in 1973. This time I would go back as an instructor, and to make things even better, I was to be promoted to Petty Officer Aircrewman (POACMN), which meant a little more money and slightly more kudos and credibility. This also meant that for the first time since Kieran had been born in 1976, I would have some time at home with Cath and the children. I would still be away, but not half as much as before, and now we had a slightly bigger family and pay packet, we could consider moving house.

One other thing was set in my mind. As a father I would do as much as I could with the limited time I had with Kieran and Simon as children. My father did absolutely nothing with me, never played or took an interest in my life or what I achieved. Consequently, I vowed to do as much as I could: play, take an interest and hopefully be a real dad. I knew I couldn't be there all the time, but what time I did have with the family would be quality time.

I joined 707 Squadron at the beginning of March, a new start as a POACMN and as an aircrewman instructor. At the same time a couple of other crewmen had joined the squadron, Steve Huxley and John 'Speedy' Ball (who had been on my BFT) both also from 845. We settled in to learn our new trade as instructors. Steve and I were newly promoted, so were quite junior to some of the more senior crewmen instructors already on the unit, even though I now had over 1,700 hours of flying experience in the SAR and commando role. The main thing, though, was that we were the only crewmen on 707 who had served in NI, so had a good deal of street cred with the students, as we had already done the job they were being trained for. By this time though, Speedy had decided to leave the Navy and start a new career with the police in Derbyshire, so six months later we all wished him good luck as he went off to start his new life in the Derbyshire hills.

Steve and I had now been instructors for some time; the flying was good, with lots of low-level and high-level flying, navigation exercises and all sorts of utility flying, like load lifting, winching, abseiling and the odd display at air shows. The hours were quite long, with lots of report writing and lesson planning, but life was good, both at work and at home. I was able to get home almost all the time, although I was still expected to night fly at least once, if not twice a week and we would be detached at least one week in every month. That was nothing compared to being on the front-line squadron, away for months on end.

Although it was great being an instructor, eventually the flying became quite monotonous. With the courses lasting ten weeks, the training became routine and repetitive and I thought I was losing the edge; yes it was still a challenge to get students through a very difficult course (the pass rate was normally around 60 per cent), but Cath could tell I was not as happy as I used to be and not quite as enthusiastic as before, becoming quite disillusioned with the routine of the job.

In March 1979 there came a bit of bad news; Lyall 'Brad' Bradbury, who I had been on POACMN's Course with, had been involved in a serious accident in Norway during the February exercise. A formation of three Wessex Mk5s had been operating near Haarstad, just near the Norwegian coast. They were flying low level, but fortunately with no troops on board. In Norway all of the wires are marked on our maps, but sometimes the logging industry erect heavy-duty cables to move their felled trees to the coast; these should be published, but on this occasion they had failed to notify the authorities and the wire was spread across the valley at about 80ft off the ground. The first aircraft flown by Lieutenant Bernard 'Bruno' Brunsden and Sub Lieutenant Herbert 'Paddy' Clarke, with Brad in the back, did not see the wire and they flew into it. The wire slid up the nose and caught between the main rotor and gearbox, flipping the aircraft onto its back. The aircraft landed upside-down, killing the two pilots instantly, the cabin was crushed, but Brad was not dead; he was badly injured, but did not survive the trip to the nearest hospital. Another sad loss of a friend and colleague.

Brad's funeral was a week later near Edinburgh. Speedy, Steve and I drove up to the funeral to be pall bearers; the occasion was especially sad as Brad's wife Lesley was heavily pregnant with their first child. We needed to practice carrying the coffin, and as we did this Speedy remarked, 'Will Brad be this heavy John?' I turned around and said, 'Brad is in the coffin, Speedy.' He was a little confused and upset about having to bury another of our mates. Brad's wife had the baby four months later and called the boy Lyle after his father.

Towards the end of 1979, I decided to see how things panned out and then see what came along job-wise. I was coming to a break point in my career. Much like Speedy had done, I now had to make a choice.

At the time the North Sea oil rigs were just starting to employ more people and there were plenty of jobs in the Shetlands as Search and Rescue aircrewmen. The pay was better and the lifestyle was stable, but housing was expensive; positives and negatives I thought. Cath and I discussed our options. She backed me in whatever I wanted to do and I was just about to resign and take the job in Scotland when, out of the blue, the Conservative government, led by Margret Thatcher, decided to give the military a 25 per cent pay rise. That put the cat among the pigeons and made my decision even harder. After much deliberation, Cath and I decided it would be best if I remained in the Navy and that we would probably move to a larger house with a garden for the children to play in.

So, the next week I signed on; first for fourteen years' service and then a week later for twenty-two years' service, that way you got two lots of re-engaging leave. A bit of a play on the rules, but everyone did it. That meant I got two months extra leave rather than one. Leave that you could take anytime up to leaving the service. Life seemed to be picking up again, but the job was to be getting me down a bit.

Cath and I put our house in Martock on the market and started looking for a new place, hopefully in a child-friendly environment. After lots of looking around we found a new-build in a village called Queen Camel, the other side of Yeovilton. The village had a primary school, doctors' surgery, a small shop and two pubs, and was only three miles from RNAS Yeovilton, which meant I could cycle to work and Cath could have the car. The house was in a small cul-de-sac with a play area out front and a playing field, about 200 yards away at the back; a great area for Kieran and Simon to grow up in. Because the house was new, there were a lot of other families with young children nearby, better for Cath and the children when I was away on duty.

Not long after moving house the Commanding Officer chose me to take the lead on instructing a new course of crewmen. A bit of a bummer at the time, as I had applied to complete the all arms course with the Royal Marines at Lympstone in Devon, which had to be forfeited. Maybe later!

These student aircrewmen were different from the rest though. The course was getting short of Navy applicants and had decided to open up our branch to the Royal Marines. The first course was due to start shortly and the boss wanted me to take the lead, which was quite an honour really. There would be seven Royal Marines on the course and my number two would be Steve Huxley (good news!).

The seven consisted of one Sergeant and two Corporals who had been Army Air Corps (AAC) trained air gunners, and four newly naval-trained Marines, who had gone through the same BFT as all the naval aircrewmen. Seven students on course at once was hard work to begin with – but not as hard as it eventually became. Steve and I had to put long hours in to get the AAC guys up to speed with our naval training. Not their fault, because their original training was aimed towards single-engine light helicopters and gunning, rather than the larger support helicopter operations and navigation the way the Navy operated.

About four weeks into the course, I got a call to help out with an aircraft delivery to Fleetlands, an aircraft maintenance base near Portsmouth. I would be flying with Steve Daniels, affectionately known as 'Boy Pilot' because he looked like an 18-year-old just out of school. He was a very good pilot though, a natural flyer and aviator. The aircraft to be delivered was a new Sea King Mk4. This newly purchased helicopter, made by Westland of Yeovil to a Sikorsky design, would eventually come into service with 846 Commando Squadron at Yeovilton. The aircraft was lovely, lots of navigation aids, long endurance and much more capable than the Wessex, which I had flown in for the past seven years.

When I got home and told Cath about the Sea King, she knew what I was about to say. 846 Squadron would soon be operating the aircraft, but would have only three to begin with and were about to start aircrew conversions from Wessex to Sea King. I asked Cath whether she would mind if I volunteered to go back to the front line on 846 and to operate the Sea King Mk4. She immediately said she didn't mind because she knew it would make me happier at work. I spoke to the boss, Lieutenant Commander Simon Thornewill, the next day, who said he would let me go with reservations, as he didn't want to lose me. I also spoke to the Chief Aircrewman (CPOACMN) of 846 Alf Tupper, my SAR Course instructor from 1975; he said he would love to have me on the unit and would clear it with Charlie Wines our drafter. I was cleared to go when the Royal Marine Aircrewman's course had been completed.

At the end of each tour a report is written about an individual's performance while on the squadron. At the beginning of my flying career, I was getting a four or five (out of ten) assessment. This report at the end of my time on 707 Squadron was quite different. My boss Lt Cdr Simon Thornewill wrote: 'A most competent and professional Petty Officer Aircrewman who is a good instructor and sets a fine example to his students.' Not bad I thought, and the write up also carried a seven assessment, the best I had ever achieved on a squadron. Only once before had I got a seven and that was on my POACMN Course in 1977.

Later that week we had a visitor to the squadron, someone I remembered well. It was my old senior pilot from 848 Squadron, the man who had said 'Sheldon, you will never make it as an aircrewman.' He was still a Lieutenant Commander, as he had been in 1972, and hadn't changed much. I was introduced to him, but he didn't recognise me – or if he did, he didn't let on. Well, there I was – one of the senior instructors on the squadron; a Petty Officer Aircrewman, passed for Chief Petty Officer. I thought, 'up yours mate! I did make it and hopefully there are better things still to come!'

A week later and the drafting signals were all completed. I would see the end of the Royal Marine course on 707 and leave to join 846 Squadron, where I would complete my Sea King Mk4 conversion. All the Royal Marines on the Operation Flying Training course passed, it was a credit to all the aircrewmen instructors on 707 that the whole course had got through, we had put in an enormous amount of time and effort to achieve a 100 per cent pass rate.

At the start of November, I left 707, carried out my joining routine and started work on 846 Squadron. Cath said there was an immediate change in my outlook to my military and flying career and a return back to my old enthusiastic attitude and zest for life. I really enjoyed the change; a new aircraft and a new squadron. Things were looking up again. We had a new house, a great family, and I had an exciting future career looking ahead to more challenging times.

Chapter 5

The squadron still had only four Sea King Mk4s, which was OK, because there were only six pilots qualified to fly them at the time. The crewmen were all doing conversion courses, which were run by my old mate Alf Tupper, the squadron CPOACMN; the training was quite intense, but really enjoyable. A change from the Wessex Mk5, this aircraft had quite a complex and modern navigation system for the time, which was fed from a Doppler and Decca input, the latter used beams from transmitters around the country which emitted lines of radio beams that crossed and located your position, which was then displayed on a Tactical Air Navigation System (TANS). This was all new to us and not everyone picked up the complexities of the system very easily. Fortunately, it was right up my street; I had been interested in it since that one flight a couple of months before with Steve.

As we progressed towards our qualification on the Mk4 Sea King, we started to use all the systems in the aircraft. It had lots of radio navigation aids, like VOR, DME, ADF and even a very basic moving map, that ran off the TANS.

One of the best things about this aircraft was that it always had to be manned by two qualified crew: a pilot and a suitably qualified left-hand seat operator (i.e., someone who could operate the manual throttles to the engines, if the engine computers failed). The crewmen were all qualified in this operation, so when we were flying, we were often in the left-hand seat due to a shortage of pilots. This was great, we would control all the navigation systems and also get to fly the beast every now and again. Lieutenant Al Davies (who I had rescued in Taranto Bay in 1974) was the lead Qualified Helicopter Instructor (QHI) pilot and was probably one of the best in the business. Al was a QHI, IRI and Test Pilot, and combined with all this he was a thoroughly nice man. He taught me to fly and I became quite good at it.

After about a month with Alf Tupper, I qualified on the Mk4 Sea King with a good pass. Combined with my recent instructional experience, I soon became one of the instructors, teaching the conversions to type for the aircrewmen. At the time the squadron also had eight Wessex Mk5s, but soon we would get more Sea Kings, which would replace the Wessex.

On the squadron was a French exchange pilot, his name was John Francois 'JF' Bazaugour. His English was OK but not great, so when I flew with him he would say in a French accent, 'You have the radio.' It worked fine, he would fly and I would do the navigation and radio. On one occasion we went to RAF Shawbury, stopped for fuel and went to the aircrew feeder (a pilots/crewman café). I had ordered fish and chips with bread and butter. I was making a chip sandwich. When JF asked me what it was, I said, 'In Liverpool they call it a chip butty.' He thought it looked good so he had one too and kept on talking about his 'chip butty'. From then on, he was always called 'Scouse Bazaugour', and he loved having his chip butties from Liverpool.

Cath really noticed a change in me, as I came home from work happy and contented. Our home life improved immensely. Kieran was now 4 years old and going to playschool in West Camel; Simon was a growing 2-year-old, always playing in the mud and getting dirty.

The flying became more intense; all the Army and Royal Marine units wanted to work with us because the aircraft was capable of much more than the Wessex. For example, the Sea King could take twenty-seven passengers, whereas the Wessex could take a maximum of only twelve, with hardly any fuel. The endurance of the Wessex was 2½ hours, whereas the Sea King Mk4 could fuel up to 6,000lbs giving an endurance of 5½ hours, quite a step up in capability for the commando units and the squadrons.

It was now February 1981, HMS *Invincible*, a carrier disguised as a through deck cruiser, was becoming operational. We were sent on board to carry out the plane guard again for the Sea Harriers. HRH Prince Charles The Prince of Wales (POW) was planned to visit and watch the Harriers operate, mainly take offs and landings. The POW had been a qualified Wessex pilot at the same time I was on 845 in 1974, so he knew what this was all about. After a few Sea Harrier landings and take-offs we took him ashore again. Scouse Bazaugour was the pilot, I suggested that we should let POW go in the left-hand seat and have a fly. He agreed and I am sure Prince Charles appreciated the chance to fly again.

The remainder of the year was taken up with training, operations and learning to use the aircraft in a tactical operating scenario. Operating day and night, low- and high-level, gunnery, load lifting, winching and fighter evasion; this was not for the fainthearted – throwing the aircraft around the skies, trying to avoid fighters trying to shoot you down. I was quite good at this, thanks to my experience on 846 in 1975; experience that would come in to good use later on in my flying career.

In September 1981, I and another POACMN, Graham McRoberts (McR), were to go on HMS *Hermes*. *Hermes* had now been converted from a commando carrier to a fixed-wing carrier, with a ski jump ramp for the Sea Harrier. We were to go on Exercise Westlant for a couple of months. This would take us up and down the East Coast of the United States, Bermuda and the Caribbean. We sailed on 2 September, four days before Cath's birthday – not a good start. Fortunately she was very happy in Queen Camel and had made a lot of friends.

After crossing the Atlantic the ship put into Mayport in Florida, we then disembarked to a US Naval airfield, Naval Air Station Jacksonville. The flying there was good and we taught US naval pilots how to do tactical recoveries of downed aircrew and inserts of special forces into the Florida Everglades, not a place to ditch or crash as it was full of alligators.

These exercises were carried out under battlefield condition with US Navy fighters giving us aircover while we carried out the missions.

After five weeks in Florida living with the US Navy, we had to move up to North Carolina. *Hermes* would sail around to Norfolk in Virginia and eventually we would fly up there and meet it. Our helicopter detachment consisted of two Sea King from 846 Squadron and also two Wessex from 845. One of the Wessex set off first, to go to the ship and then on to New River, the US Marine Corps Base, from where we would eventually operate. Unfortunately, as the Wessex was coming in to the coast near South Carolina, it had a main transmission failure (i.e. loss of all power to the main rotors) and when this happens the only way is down. The pilot, Lieutenant Doyne Ditmus, auto-rotated down to the sea (this is much like a sycamore leaf floating down, using the airflow through the blades to maintain rotor speed until the last second, when the pilot uses that momentum to slow the aircraft's descent and land softly). He did a really good job and all the crew and passengers got out. Most of them were picked up, with their kit, by local fishermen and the rest by us when we arrived on the scene not long after the incident. After returning to the ship to report what had happened, the boss of the Air Department on the ship (Commander Air (Wings)) was a bit agitated. Apparently, there were still some secret documents on the aircraft. I explained to Wings that the water was very shallow and the tail of the aircraft was still sticking up, clear of the surface and if we had a diver we could recover the documents.

One of the Air Department (Lieutenant Joe Cannon) was a volunteer, he was also an ex-SAR Diver and had worked with me at Portland in 1975. His currency qualification was still in date for diving and SAR jumping from a helicopter. We briefed and lifted to do the recovery; I would despatch Joe by the Wessex's tail and he would dive down and recover the documents – easy, we thought! We arrived on top of the Wessex; Joe got ready, I checked his gear and he sat in the doorway of the Sea King, I positioned the Sea King so Joe could jump into the sea and then go straight into the Wessex main doorway.

The Sea King was now in a low hover, about 20ft, and Joe gave me the thumbs up. I gave him two taps on his shoulder and he was away. He landed in the water, resurfaced and gave me the thumbs up, to say he was OK and would now dive down into the Wessex. All went well, until I saw several black fins arriving around the ditched Wessex. As some people know, the beat of a helicopter's rotors is like a calling card for sharks and these were great whites – the nasty ones. Joe was now in the belly of the Wessex, unaware that there were about twenty sharks all around him. The only communication we had with a diver in those days was by thunder flash (a large firework-banger). I thought that if I threw a couple of thunder flashes into the water, it might scare the sharks off and also bring Joe to the surface. It sort of worked, after five thunder flashes the sharks moved away – but only by about 50 yards. Joe came to the surface and I waved and pointed to the sharks; he saw them, climbed up the tail of the Wessex and sat there like a pixie on top of a mushroom. There was no way he was going back into the water because the sharks had started to come back to the ditched aircraft and under our rotors. Joe signalled to be picked up and I lowered the winch and strop to recover him into the Sea King; thankfully he had done the job and recovered the documents, so Wings was a happy man when we landed back on *Hermes*. I wish I had taken a camera though, to get the photograph of Joe on the tail of the Wessex – a missed opportunity!

The flight to USMC Base New River and the Camp Lejeune complex was achieved without hitch, but with only three aircraft now. The men who had gone down in the ditching of the Wessex had got all their kit back from the fishermen and made their way up to join us, in our new detachment location. The military area was huge, about half the size of Wales, with ranges where you could fire any weapon from small arms to 16-inch guns, also a coastal range and, to the west of Camp Lejeune, US Marine airfields and troop camps. The Marines really looked after us, we carried out a couple of small exercises with them and our small detachment of Royal Marines and at the end of each exercise, it was drinks and BBQ time. After ten days with the US Marines, it was decided to have a full-on sports day. This included American football, rugby and deck hockey.

We started with American football on the beach, some of the opposition came out with helmets and pads on, we had T-shirts and shorts! Most of us had only seen American Football on TV before, so we learned how to play on the hoof. We did OK for ourselves without too many injuries; we did get beaten, but not thrashed. Rugby next – this was a different matter, no helmets or pads for anyone. As a team of sailors, we had previously played rugby together. The Yanks did not like the physical contact without their pads on and obviously we came down easy on them (my foot we did!). We hit them as hard as we could, I think they had a new respect for rugby players, because at that time not many people played the game in the United States. We beat them quite convincingly; mind you I was also the playing ref.

After all that exercise, it was time to eat and I must say they laid on a great spread, with a pig roast (a whole pig!). Lots of other food and beer, what a good meal. After the food and beer had settled down, it was time to play Deck Hockey (a naval form of hockey, played on the deck of a ship, with a puck made of rope, covered in black masking tape and a stick made of a bit of branch about 3ft long, with a slight turn at the end). One bit of advice I gave the opposition was to wear some boots and that there were no rules. They didn't take the advice about boots or about there being no rules. It was carnage, after about five minutes three of the Marines had been carted off to the med centre, with cuts to hands and heads. I stopped the game and made it clear about the rules, or the lack of them. Eventually they got the hang of it, but by that time we had beaten them, with no time for a comeback. The Marines took the day in good spirits and we all ended up in the bar for the final competition, a boat race! Drinks are lined up either side of a long table with a team of eight guys each side. The object is to drink all the beers one at a time, the first to finish wins. A good night was had by all.

After a couple more days at New River, we flew to Norfolk Naval Base, the biggest military port of the eastern coast of the US. There we re-embarked on HMS *Hermes*.

On arrival in Norfolk, we called the ship on the radio and discovered that we had to land before the ship came alongside; this we did, just before the ship entered harbour. The aircraft were ranged on the upper deck; we stayed on the flight deck to see the views of the port as we came alongside. The ship was to be berthed next to the USS *Dwight D Eisenhower*, one of the massive American aircraft carriers. HMS *Hermes* was the biggest ship in the Royal Navy, but we were dwarfed by the ship next door. I had spent three days on *Dwight D Eisenhower* a couple of months previously and it was mammoth, with 6,000 crew and about 120 fixed- and rotary-wing aircraft on board. When you went down to the lower decks it was advised that you went as a group because the centre of the ship was like a ghetto, controlled by sailors who ran the lower decks as their own and to be avoided by strangers. Although our ship was smaller with fewer aircraft, I preferred it to the large American ship.

In Norfolk, I played some rugby for the HMS *Hermes* first team and had a couple of runs ashore. Then we were off again heading back out to the Atlantic and across to Bermuda, where we had another couple of rugby matches against some exile players and the police force, who showed us the highlights of the island after the match. I'm glad they did! They showed us where not to go – the place was so expensive that I couldn't have afforded to drink out there for very long. The island was lovely though, great beaches and golf courses, but very windy.

The ship set sail again, this time to Tortola in the British Virgin Islands, while in Tortola the detachment disembarked and had ten days under canvas in tents, operating with our company of young Royal Marines. The day before the intended disembarkation, I went ashore with the flight commander in a Sea King to do a recce. We landed at Beef Island, Tortola's main airport. There I bumped into a Mr Charles Tobias, who was just about to fly out, but wanted a look around our Sea King. Charles was the founder of the Pussers Rum Company and as we chatted he said he would contact me when he returned two days later and invite me round for dinner. He was true to his word and McR and I went for dinner. He also arranged an exiles rugby match and came to our camp site with two crates of Pussers rum to be divided out among the men. We had a great TOT time that night.

The only downer on the trip was that our army exchange REME sergeant, a man called Chalky White, went swimming one night after the Pina Colada tall ships yacht race and never returned. We got airborne and searched all day for him, but never found him. There was speculation that he had been attacked by a shark, or hit by a boat. Others thought that he had just been employed as a yacht's captain to sail around the Caribbean, due to the fact he possessed a Yachting Captain's sailing ticket and was a qualified marine engineer. Who knows, but we never saw him again.

The day the detachment was to end and re-embark on HMS *Hermes*, Charles returned with a truck. There were a hundred Royal Marines and about sixty of us in the helicopter detachment and Charles provided a bottle of Pussers rum for each and every one of us. What a fantastic gift and send off.

The ship got back to the UK mid-December. It had been a really enjoyable detachment but also a long one, so I was glad to get back to Cath and the children for Christmas leave at home.

Chapter 6

The first three months of 1982 were taken up by routine tasks. I did the AR5 aircrew gas mask course and learned how to operate as aircrew with a special gas mask on. Then a couple of detachments to Scotland to work with 45 Commando and some SBS tasking at Poole.

By now the squadron was all Sea King Mk4, with the last Wessex leaving at the end of 1981. The last aircrew conversions were taking place in Norway and then the whole squadron would be back together by the end of March. Easter leave took place as normal and we returned to work refreshed and ready to take on whatever came next.

Well, what came next was very much unexpected. At the end of March, the Argentinians had taken up station off the coast of South Georgia and then put some men on the island; this was their first step to the eventual invasion of the Falkland Islands. At the beginning of April, the full invasion took place and a British Sovereign island had been taken over. The call went out to all squadron personnel to return immediately. I lived only three miles away and was back within minutes, as were the personnel who lived on board at RNAS Yeovilton.

The preparations started for us to embark as soon as possible. The aircraft were made ready and all our kit was gathered together for the long trip south. I knew where the Falkland Islands were, but quite a few didn't have a clue where we were going; 8,000 miles down to the South Atlantic was a good guess! By 5 April all were ready to embark. Those who could went home to say their goodbyes and have a last night at home before potentially going off to war. I say 'potentially' because even then, some thought it would not come to conflict and that the Argentine government would back down and leave the island. That was not to happen though, and so on 6 April we embarked four aircraft onto HMS *Fearless*, four on to HMS *Intrepid* and another four on to HMS *Hermes*. One more aircraft was due from the Westland Helicopter Company and would be stripped and made ready to be flown in the back of a Belfast transport aircraft to Ascension Island, where it would be put back together and flown on to *Hermes*.

Cath, to my delight, was quite upbeat about my going away, or at least she put on a very brave face. I know she was crying when she dropped me off that morning as I said goodbye to her, Kieran and Simon. This time we had no idea when, or possibly even if, I would come back. A different situation to anything Cath had experienced before. Of course, in those days there were no mobile phones or internet, the only communication was via snail mail in the guise of what was called a BLUEY. A single paged letter that was free to send, but it also took about a week or so to get to the recipient. A long time when you haven't a clue what is going on at home or in the South Atlantic 8,000 miles away.

We embarked early on that very dreary April morning with a low-visibility approach; even getting to the ship was tasking, but we all arrived safely, got our kit down to the mess deck and settled in for the long voyage south.

The ship was full to the gunnels with weapons, food, aircraft, vehicles and most of all men! The ship was packed, with men sleeping in every available space and on the way south the training was intense. The old adage, 'train hard fight easy', kept coming to mind. The flight deck was also full with four Sea Kings and three Scout helicopters from 3 Brigade Air Squadron of the Royal Marines.

The tanks' deck was heaving with vehicles and the light tanks of the Blues and Royals. The task force would make its way to Ascension Island where it would stop and carry out a stores/personnel shuffle between all the ships; loading had happened so quickly that a lot of kit and men were in the wrong location and it had to be sorted out before going further south to the Falklands.

As we arrived at Ascension we were told that the Argentinians were not going anywhere and therefore we would be going to war. Cross-decking of stores and personnel continued and then a group of ships, including HMS *Hermes* and HMS *Sheffield*, left early to start the long trip south.

Most of the stores transfers and beach training had now been completed and the remainder of the fleet would leave in the following two days to catch up with *Hermes* and the fleet for a future landing in the Falkland Islands.

It was now 23 April, I was ashore on Ascension Island with Tim Kelly and Ian 'Robby' Robertson, when we heard that one on our aircraft from *Hermes* had crashed while doing some cross-decking between a Royal Fleet Auxiliary ship and *Hermes*. The weather had deteriorated and the cloud base reduced. The aircraft was being flown by a single pilot, and POACMN

Ben Casey was the crewman. The pilot, Flight Lieutenant Bob Grundy, had made a radio call to *Hermes* for another pilot and was about to approach to land when due to the low visibility he flew into the water. Bob managed to get out of the wreckage, but Ben had been killed instantly on impact. The helicopter had broken up on striking the surface and Ben was lost to the ocean. His body was never recovered and he was the first casualty of the Falklands War. Another sombre day and a reality check for us all, that we were going to war and some of us may not return. A small service was held for Ben that afternoon.

We sailed the next day and made our way south. More pre-conflict training took place, some of the crews learnt how to use the new night vision goggles the squadron had obtained from the trials unit at Farnborough; there was a good deal of shooting – from the aircraft and on the ground; parachuting and operating with the Special Forces we had on board; resistance to interrogation training, and learning about the Argentine forces, what ships and aircraft they had and what air defence systems they could employ against us. We also had a brief about the flora and fauna of the Falklands, given by Major Ewen Southby-Tailyour RM. He had been the detachment commander in the Falklands some years before, so was the resident specialist on the Islands. As he was giving us the lecture about the wildlife, all the crewmen were sat at the back, our normal position for some reason (the crewman's option). He was telling us about seals and said that Leopard Seals were the dangerous ones; they capture penguins in their mouths and then shake them so violently that the penguin is shaken out of its skin. At that, Allan 'Splash' Ashdown, who was sat next to me, piped up and said, 'Excuse me sir, I always take the wrapper off my penguins before I eat them too.' The whole audience burst out laughing, but Major Southby-Tailyour did not see the funny side of it at all. I thought his face would crack! It was a bit of humour during quite a tense time!

As we progressed towards the Falklands, the island of South Georgia was taken back from Argentine control. Two Wessex Mk5s from 845 Squadron were lost while trying to recover the special forces assault team from the glacier on South Georgia, but thankfully there no injuries. The recovery was completed eventually by Lieutenant Commander Ian Stanley and his crew in a Wessex Mk3 from HMS *Glamorgan*, it was a fantastic piece of flying and Ian was decorated for his achievements that day.

Our leaders had come up with an invasion plan to take back the Falklands, but prior to that our other squadron detachment based in HMS *Hermes* had been inserting SAS/SBS on to the Islands during night covert operations.

CHAPTER 6

One of these Sea Kings callsign VC was also flown to Chile via Argentina to insert SAS on the Argentine mainland. The aircraft was then finally landed in Chile where the crew destroyed it by setting the Sea King on fire with the signal flare from the back of the aircraft, this was so that the Chileans and Argentinians would not know where the aircraft had come from and would not suspect that a special forces unit had been dropped off prior to the aircraft having been ditched . That was two aircraft of 846 and two aircraft of 845 Squadron we had already lost and the main assault had not yet happened.

The cross-decking continued; on 19 May I was flying with the boss, Simon Thornewill, and the night was about as black as it could be, no starlight at all and very low cloud. We had just landed on *Fearless* when a call came in that another Sea King Mk4 which had been ferrying SAS soldiers from *Hermes* to *Intrepid* had crashed. It was very dark, with a heavy sea and the aircraft had flown into the sea on final approach. No one really knows exactly what happened, but the aircraft had broken in half on impact with the sea and started to sink. There were thirty people on board, three of them crew. Of those thirty, twenty died that night: eighteen SAS, one army soldier and the aircrewman Corporal Michael 'Doc' Love RM, who I had taken through training a couple of years before. This was the biggest loss of life in one incident for a long, long time. Two crewmen from 846 squadron were now dead and three aircraft lost, where would it end?

Two days later, on 21 May, was our D-Day. The weather was awful again, which actually helped us get into San Carlos Water, a bay on the west coast of East Falkland, without any air strikes from the Argentine Air Force. The landings took place, with no land opposition, which was a good thing.

That day I flew nine hours, mainly taking stores, 105 light guns and Rapier missile systems to the shore. Later in the afternoon the weather cleared and the Argentine Air Force started hitting us from the skies. There were A4 Skyhawk and Mirage jet fighter-bombers and also Pucara ground-attack aircraft. They were very brave and flew in to San Carlos at ultra-low level to drop their bombs. Some hit their targets, some not. Fortunately for us, because they were so low, some of the bombs had no time to arm themselves before they hit the ships and failed to explode.

On 23 May HMS *Antelope* was bombed and an unexploded bomb lodged in the centre of the ship. The bomb disposal team worked hard, but the bomb exploded and blew off one man's arm. Later I took him to the hospital ship *Uganda*. On getting him into the aircraft he asked me to be careful because he only had one arm; I promised him I would be as careful as I could. The ship exploded in the evening a day or so later, and it was a sight you don't ever want to see; a sight I will never forget.

As the war continued, we worked hours on end, day and night. I had never flown so many hours in such a short period of time before. It was now 25 May – Simon's birthday, he was 4 years old and I was away again. The day was taken up with tasking, and a few airstrikes from the Argentinians, then we got a call over the HF (High Frequency Radio) that HMS *Coventry* had been bombed about ten miles north of Pebble Island in West Falkland. All available helicopters were to attend ASAP. Our crew, comprising Lieutenant Bill Fewtrell, Alf Tupper and I, took off immediately. I put the position into the TANS and we set off, keeping a good lookout for fighters. We saw one and watched as it got closer, then recognised it as one of ours, a Sea Harrier, our luck was in! We set best speed and it took about seven minutes to get to the ship. Alf and I prepared to carry out the rescue and as we arrived we saw a lot of dinghies in the water, but most disturbing was the sight of the ship. It was starting to roll on its side and would soon turn turtle. The men in the dinghies were OK for the moment, so we searched for any survivors on their own away from the ship; we only found one body, that of a laundryman. We had to recover him, so Alf and I tossed a coin and he went down on the winch wire to recover the body. I brought Alf and the laundryman into the cabin and tried to resuscitate him but there was no hope, so we put him in the jump seat and went to recover the living.

There were a series of dinghies tied together, but the ship, which had now turned turtle, looked a sorry sight. Alf said he would go down and manage the men in the dinghies, so I put him into the first dinghy and I started recovering *Coventry*'s crew. The first was a Sub Lieutenant and I found out later he was the brother of a friend, then came another eighteen, most with burns and other injuries. By this time more aircraft had arrived and ours was getting full. I said to Alf that it was time to go, but he wanted to stay and manage the dinghy rescue. So, I put him back down and we returned to the mainland with the casualties. Alf was awarded a DSM for his action and he deserved it.

The sight of HMS *Coventry* turning over will always be in my mind though, and I hope never to have to see the likes again. Bill and I landed on the stores ship RFA *Fort Austin* and after the casualties and walking wounded were taken off we refuelled and then took the body of the laundryman over to the Red Beach field hospital in Ajax Bay. There we were met by Commander Rick 'Doc' Jolly, a legend in the SAR and medical world. I had first met him in NI and now he was the leader of what became the Red and Green life machine. On 27 May the field hospital was hit by a 500lb bomb, but in spite of this the surgeons carried on saving lives.

On one occasion a crewman was lifting a load full of NAAFI sweets and nutty bars when the load became unstable and he had to jettison it onto the ground. All the crewmen from 846 had the grid reference of where it had been dropped, so we would land and stock up every chance we had. I know it was naughty, but the load couldn't be recovered, so we had to save it from going to waste.

After all the flying we had done over the past few weeks the aircraft needed a deal of deep maintenance. Our aircraft call sign VA (ZA298) was programmed to go to RFA *Fort Austin* to have one of the engines changed. Lieutenant Dave Lord and I flew the aircraft over to *Fort Austin* at last light so the engineers could complete the work. After dropping off the aircraft, folding it and stowing it in the hangar, we got picked up in another Sea King flown by Bill Fewtrell and Corporal Christopher 'Lel' Lelittka to take us back to HMS *Fearless*. We boarded the aircraft and as it was only a five-minute transit, Dave stood up behind the front-left seat and I sat in the back with Lel. It was dark now and we didn't have any NVG, so flew the aircraft on instruments and visual night flying. We took off and circuited to *Fearless* and as we did so, Bill and Dave started talking about some lights to the left (shades of Bill Sample and Norman Lees a few years before). As they discussed the lights the aircraft descended towards the water, at that point Lel, who was looking out of the back-left window, shouted 'UP, UP, UP!' Bill pulled in the collective lever and we climbed away from the water. Lel had seen the anti-collision light reflecting on the water and Bill saw the radio altimeter climb back up through 10ft as he climbed the aircraft back to 500ft. Another close shave and we were very lucky that Lel had seen the reflection on the water.

On the night of 31 May, HMS *Fearless* returned from picking up 5 Brigade from the QE2, which had sailed down with 5 Brigade re-enforcements of the Scots and Welsh Guards and also the Ghurkhas. As we had not been on board for a hot shower and food for some four days, the boss decided we could spend the night on board and the engineers could check the aircraft over while Alf, Simon, Dave and myself plus our engineers could get some rest and hot food.

There were a few explosions during the night, but no one on board knew where, or what they were. In the morning we were all refreshed, fed and watered, and had even managed to have a beer for the first time in a while. The aircraft's minor faults were all fixed, so we manned up and started the aircraft to take the engineers back to our tent site in a little gully on the east side of San Carlos Water. When we arrived, the site was carnage; our 12ft x 12ft green tent was in tatters, a deep bomb crater had appeared about 5ft from the entrance to the tent, or where the entrance had been. Shrapnel was everywhere. During the night while we were on the ship, a Canberra bomber (ex-British) had come along, presumably trying to bomb the task force ships, but had missed and run a line about 1,000 yards to the east, straight over the top of the squadron's forward operating bases. Our tent was the only one destroyed and if we had not gone on board the previous night, we would all have been killed. We now had to go back on to the ship and get a replacement tent and equipment so we could continue with the war. I managed to salvage a lump of shrapnel, to bring home; it's now mounted on a nice piece of oak and a constant reminder of that night and another close call.

The Royal Marine artillery battery, 29 Commando, were pushing forward each day as the troops moved closer to the east and the capital, Stanley. One of our main jobs was to lift and shift the guns and ammunition forward to provide fire to cover the troops advance. The flying was tiring with long hours. On one occasion I was flying with Lieutenant John Miller and Splash Ashdown, we normally had two pilots up front due to the chance of being hit by aircraft or small arms fire, but this day only John was flying up front and he was getting really tired; I jumped into the left-hand seat to give him a break, I could fly quite well and he needed a rest. We dropped off one gun and then returned for the next. I took over the controls as we flew the aircraft back to the pick-up location. As we transited back, John Miller fell asleep. I told Splash what was happening and asked whether it was OK with him if we let John sleep and did this ourselves. He was OK with that, so we ran in to pick up the next gun. I came to the hover, Splash marshalled me over the load, it was hooked on and we slowly lifted the gun. The transit back to the drop point was uneventful and the run in was OK, Splash voice-marshalled me over the drop point. The gun was about 2ft above the ground when the gunners came and turned the gun to point where they wanted it, and we put the load down on the ground. When the gunners had released the load, Splash and I went around again. Next load was ammunition, and we did one more load after that before John woke up. We told him what we had done and he was fine with it, he understood our capabilities – and we had not crashed the aircraft, that was the good thing!

The next few days were taken up with moving forward, the Royal Marines were doing the famous Yomp from Port San Carlos to Stanley.

CHAPTER 6

The Paras and Scots Guards were moving forward south of the main range of mountains between Goose Green and Fitzroy and the Welsh Guards were being sailed round to Bluff Cove just by Fitzroy in RFA *Sir Galahad* and RFA *Sir Tristram*. All this was to get ready for the push to take Stanley, as the weather the week before had been appalling with snow, rain, sleet, strong winds and low cloud.

On 8 June, we had been flying around San Carlos Water, when a call came in to go to Bluff Cove, where *Sir Galahad* and *Tristram* were anchored up. An air-raid had taken place and both ships had been bombed by a series of strikes by A4 Skyhawks and two Mirages. There were many casualties and speed was of the essence, so we set off at high speed. Simon Thornewill was flying and we were doing about 120 knots going over the ridge between San Carlos and Goose Green at very low level because there was still a major air threat. As we crested the ridge, there was a loud bang and the aircraft shook. I was standing by the front port door, which had flown open and banged against the lower part of the airframe; at first we thought we had been hit by a missile, but it was simply the door coming open when the aircraft flexed as it flew over the ridge. I asked Simon to slow down, got a rope out that was attached to a rotor blade tip sock, pulled the door up and roped it off so that we could continue to Bluff Cove. When we got to the area of the two LSLs (Landing Ship Logistic) we saw smoke billowing out of both ships. There were lifeboats everywhere and quite a few Sea Kings and a Wessex hovering, going in and out of the smoke, while ammunition was still exploding. Flames were coming out of the main super-structure of the two ships with confusion everywhere.

We were told to land on the north shore of Bluff Cove, where we started getting the injured and burns survivors into the aircraft. Alf and I got as many in the cabin as we could. I don't think we even counted them in, we just got in as many as we could, then it was off to Ajax Bay and the Red Beach field hospital. En route, Alf and I tended to the wounded, gave them as many liquids as they could take and kept them as warm as we could. They were all in shock. On arrival at Ajax Bay, Doc Jolly met the aircraft as usual, Alf and I briefed Doc as much as we could about the soldiers' injuries and we then did a second run, to bring more casualties back. The ships burned for days after, becoming another one of those abiding memories. I went back there in 2016 for a battlefield tour and briefed the other members of the Commando Helicopter tour group on what it was like that day. I could still visualise the scene, even though it was thirty-four years later. It brought a shiver to my spine.

After dark we landed at our FOB site in San Carlos and let the engineers have the aircraft to fix. They had managed to get a second-hand door from one of the broken blue Sea King Mk5s of 825 Squadron; they changed the door that night and we flew round for the rest of the war with a blue door on.

The main assault to the east of Stanley was now taking place, the Royal Marines from the north, and the 2/3 Para with the rest of the army units supporting them to the south west. Mount Kent to the west of Stanley was a particular problem, hostile and well-fortified.

On 13 June, we were in Sea King Mk4 ZA298 (VA) and had been tasked to support 29 CDO again, they were giving covering fire to the attack on Mount Kent. We had just resupplied a load of ammunition to 29 Battery and were on our way back to Teal Inlet where stores were coming in for resupply. The sky was clear and conditions were quite nice for once. I was the only one listening to the HF radio, which broadcast any incoming air raids or contacts. As we set out for Teal, I heard over the HF radio that four A4 Skyhawks were heading from Mount Kent to Teal Inlet.

I was in the back-left window and immediately looked back and left toward Mount Kent. I saw the first two A4s bearing down on us and immediately called for the boss, who was flying the aircraft, to break left. Without hesitation he heaved the aircraft left and down. The first two A4s started their attack. They fired their cannons at us and flew over the top. The second pair came over us, also firing. We had been an opportunity target and after firing, the A4s left to go and bomb Teal Inlet, we had survived a fighter attack. All that training over the years, hours of fighter evasion exercises and briefs, had paid off and saved our lives.

We flew up a small gully called Impassable Valley, where we landed to check the aircraft. The helicopter was shut down, the rotors stopped. Alf and I got out, Alf with the GPMG Machine gun and I with my cooker and pan to make a brew – which seemed the right thing to do at the time, as we were going to be on the ground for a while. We set up a defensive position and waited, as we were still in enemy territory. The boss then confirmed that we had been hit; a 20mm cannon shell had gone through the main spar of one of the main rotor blades, about a third of the way out from the main hub. This was the main area of lift, so we were very lucky it hadn't snapped with all the power and pressure applied to it while we evaded. After a moment of reflection, we said at least Westland Helicopters manufacture very good blades.

It was impossible to fly with the damaged blade, so after a radio call we waited for another aircraft to come out from HMS *Fearless* with an engineering team and new rotor blade. The engineers then took off the damaged blade and replaced it with a new one. Two hours after the incident, we were back in the air. Back in the fight! The section of rotor blade where the round had pierced was later cut out and is now in the Fleet Air Arm Museum on display, as is ZA298, the most famous of the Sea King Mk4 aircraft in the fleet.

The surrender of the Argentinians to the British forces came on 15 June. We were tasked to go and get the Argentinian force leader, General Menendez, from Stanley racecourse. His troops were in tatters, soiled and underfed. Most were conscripts, as the regulars had left the Islands not long before the surrender. General Menendez on the other hand, was well dressed, with a warm coat, well fed, and arrogant in defeat.

After the surrender, most of our squadron moved to operate out of the racecourse or on board *Fearless*, which had now moved to Stanley harbour.

By this time, our crew consisted of Simon Thornewill, Lieutenant Pete Rainey, Alf and me. As we had this crew composition we were tasked to go and recover the two Argentine A109 helicopters which had been abandoned at Stanley racecourse. Fortunately, both Simon Thornewill and Pete Rainey were test pilots, so we planned to fly the two A109s back to *Fearless* and take them back to the UK.

After checking the 109s for booby traps and clearing the cabins of grenades and weapons, we were satisfied that they were OK to fly. The Argentinians had left the manuals for the aircraft in the glove compartment; that was nice of them.

The plan was that the boss and Alf would fly the first A109 back to *Fearless* and then Pete and I would deliver second one. Pete and I took Alf and Simon over to the racecourse in our Sea King. The first transit of the A109 went without a problem; then we picked up Alf and Simon from HMS *Fearless* and went back to the racecourse to recover the second A109. Pete and I were dropped off and we manned the second A109, while Simon and Alf flew the Sea King back to *Fearless*. We manned the A109 but discovered we could not communicate through our helmets as they were incompatible with the Argentinian aircraft, so we had to shout to each other from across the cockpit. The number two engine had a slight problem and would only go up to 80 per cent power. After a couple of power checks we decided between ourselves that it would be OK for the short flight to *Fearless*.

Pete started the engines, I did all the checks and we took off. The aircraft was small, but perfectly formed. It had a weapons platform on either side on which were mounted rockets and machine guns. We flew the long way around to *Fearless* (it was two miles away and it took us fifty minutes to get there) as Pete wanted to test out the aircraft. The A109 flew really nicely; it handled well and even with the lack of power was quite quick. About halfway through the trip, Pete decided he would check out the attack profile as if firing the weapons. In the harbour was a British LCT (Landing Craft Tank), a fairly large vessel that still was armed to the teeth with self-defence guns. Pete pulled up and was just rolling into an attack profile, when I said, 'this is not a good idea Peter, we are in an armed Argentinian aircraft, the crew of that vessel don't know we are British and the war has just ended. They might still be trigger happy and start shooting at us.' He agreed and turned away. We landed safely on *Fearless* and put the two A109s away for when we got home. The intercom leads were changed so that our helmets fitted and worked; next time we flew the aircraft we could talk to each other and use the radios.

Around 22 June, the clear up of the Islands had begun and it was time for 846 Squadron to leave on *Fearless* and *Intrepid*, and later, *Hermes*. The trip back via Ascension Island took until 13 July. We kept fit doing some circuit training and running around the deck, getting a good suntan and playing a few games and competitions. One of these competitions was to build a kite and the prize was a crate of beer, so Splash and I entered. The whole ship got into this and all sorts of shapes and sizes of kite appeared. Some were small and light, some medium-sized, and then there was ours: 6ft high and a good 3ft wide, made of a survival kip sheet and light metal aerial poles. It was decided that on the day of the race, the ship would slow down; that was fine for the small kites, but not for ours. All the other kites had been flown and when it was our turn, I phoned the bridge and asked the officer of the watch to speed up, or else our kite would not fly. When we finally got it airborne, there were five of us holding the kite line; it was a real flyer, but difficult to hold, so we had to reel it in. Even so, we did win the crate of ale and to this day, it was one of the largest kites I have ever seen fly off the back end of a ship.

At last we arrived back in UK waters; the weather was nice, but we didn't know what to expect when we got home. We had been away when all the news and programmes had been broadcast about the war, a patriotic nation with people full of admiration for what the task force had achieved in so short a time. Obviously, it was not joy for all; the families of the lost and injured would be grieving. Three of my fellow crewmen, Ben Casey, Doc Love and Colin Vickers had died when HMS *Glamorgan* was hit by an Exocet, launched from a flatbed lorry near the coast of the Falklands.

CHAPTER 6

On 13 July we made ready to depart for Yeovilton from *Fearless*. The aircraft would fly off and the ship would enter port at Portsmouth later the next day. The flight made ready to go, four Sea Kings and two Argentinian A109s, one with 846 markings on and the other in 3 BAS markings. Simon and Alf would fly one, Pete and I would fly the other and we would both lead the flight back over Yeovilton to announce we had returned. As we approached the landing point at Yeovilton, we could see hundreds of people waving us in. I knew Cath would be there, but not at the front – she avoids the limelight. When we had taxied in and shut the aircraft down, wives and families were running to meet their loved ones. I looked for Cath and the children and eventually saw them. I knelt down and gave Kieran and Simon a big hug and then the same for Cath. It was great to see them again and get back safe and sound. As I gave Simon and Kieran a hug a cameraman took a photograph, it was a great shot and everyone who sees it thinks the same. I have it now as a poster picture on the wall in the hallway of our house, it is one of my prized possessions.

The homecoming was wonderful, there were banners out everywhere – and then I saw the press and TV coverage; I hadn't realised the country was so much behind us. But now all I wanted to do was have some time with my family. Not talk about what had gone on, but that doesn't happen does it? Others want to know what it was like. They kept on asking and in the end, I told them about the horrors of war, what we had seen and been through, the blood and the guts, death and carnage, until eventually they didn't ask anymore, which was fine with me. It was not until later that I found out the children at Kieran's school had said to Kieran that I had died and was not coming home. I really felt for him; he had been so upset when he got home to Cath that night. Children can be so cruel at times.

A week or so later most of the squadron did a fundraising run from King Alfred's Tower to the Podymore Inn. This was to raise money for Ben and Doc's families. It was eighteen miles and we had not trained for any long distance running just short circuits on our return journey. Everyone was in pain at the end of the run, but we raised over £4,500 in Ben and Doc's memory; as well as giving money to their families we also commissioned a painting to go in the FAA museum. Afterwards, we had a few drinks in the bar in Ben and Doc's memory.

Every November we go to the Cenotaph as an Aircrewman Association and march; I think of those men who did not come home with us, and plant a cross in their memory.

The rest of 1982 was quite relaxed, after summer leave the squadron carried on training. After the Falklands, the technique for night flying changed with the use of Night Vision Goggles (NVG). Now we could see at night and fly at low level in the dark, which would give us an advantage; especially for Special Forces operations in the future.

I was now a senior aircrewman and the next step in the promotion ladder would be CPOACMN, but to get there and be confirmed in the rate/rank I needed to complete the Petty Officers Leadership Course at HMS *Royal Arthur*, a land-base establishment near Bath in Somerset. Qualifying on the leadership course with a good pass would help my promotion chances in the future.

The leadership course lasted six weeks and consisted of lessons and lectures by the staff, lessons by the students, and lots of marching and exercises (games, drill, practical leadership tests), and a final exercise in the Black Mountains. This was to last three days and nights, walking around the Welsh hills and camping overnight, with points collected for making deadlines and navigation points. I was the leader for the Black Mountain phase, with four other Petty Officers; they were pretty good, but the weather was not! It was blowing a gale, snowing and cold. We began climbing the first hill, when one of the POs (we'll call him Steve) said he was cold; I told him he should put more clothing on and we continued climbing. He said again that he was cold, so I asked if he had brought the correct gear; he had. When we got to the top of the ridge, he said again that he was so cold. I looked at him and thought maybe he was coming down with hypothermia, I couldn't take any chances as I had seen it many times before, so we erected a small tent and I got one of the other guys to get into a sleeping bag with him. I was still not sure whether Steve was just pulling my leg and being a slacker! My personal opinion was he just didn't want to be there and was trying to pull the wool over everyone's eyes, some would say he had a 'lack of moral fibre'.

After about an hour all was good. We were on a strict timetable to make our points tally so the tent came down and we started again, we continued along the ridge, then another short climb. At the top of the hill Steve started complaining again; I looked at him and checked him over. I was sure he was OK, so I told him to man up and get his act together. We carried on a little further, when he started again. This time there was a cairn nearby, I took him around the back of the Kern and gave a stern talking to.

He seemed OK and we carried on, but then he started to complain again, and I wondered if perhaps he did have a problem. My thoughts were that

I couldn't lose this man – not good leadership. I told the others we had to get down out of these appalling conditions and get to a phone. The navigation was OK, with map and compass, as I had done lots of this before on the ground and in the air.

We descended the hill and reached the road in the valley. After finding a phone, I called the HQ and spoke to our course leader, Lieutenant Commander Colin Sams (the boss). He wanted to pick Steve up, but I said no, we would stay together as a group and he would walk back. It was about fifteen miles back by road, a long yomp and heavy on the feet, especially in boots. We got back about five hours later; most of the men were OK, but Steve had blisters all over his feet. I chatted with Colin and told him the story. Later we were called in for the debrief of the exercise with the boss. He was asking the group what had gone on. The boss asked if I had done a good job as the leader of the group; all agreed I had, even Steve. Then Colin asked me if I had hit Steve, I said that I hadn't. He then asked Steve whether I had hit him, he too said no. Not the done thing, hitting your men; even in those days bullying was not a good form of leadership and could be a punishable offence.

The course ended with a big parade. We had been given a lot of good advice about leadership, the processes towards promotion and the divisional system. The lads on the course were really good, most put a lot into it and got a lot out of it – even Steve! I met him a few years later, on HMS *Invincible*, he was still a PO whereas I had been promoted to CPO; we spoke to one another but only a little, there was no reminder of what had gone on previously.

Back to 846 Squadron and normal flying again, then all the squadron were called together, and we were presented with our South Atlantic medals by Lieutenant Commander Simon Thornewill the Commanding Officer of the squadron. Two medals now – perhaps I'll get a long service medal after fifteen years' service if I'm a good boy, then I'd have almost a chest full. A few changes had taken place on the squadron by this time; Alf Tupper had been promoted and received his DSM as did Pete Imrie, who was in the Chile aircraft, and Doc Love who died in the SAS aircraft.

Chapter 7

By 24 January 1983 we were preparing to depart to Norway. Not Northern Norway this time but Southern Norway, to work with the SBS and units of 42 Commando in a place called Gardermoen, not far from Oslo. POACMN Colin Tattersall, Corporal Lel Lellitka RM and I were going on this detachment together and the flight would take us through Holland, Germany, Denmark and then across the straits to Norway.

Our flying would cover all Southern Norway from Trondheim, out to Bergen and as far south as Kristiansand. It was the 40th anniversary of the Allied raid on the heavy water plant at Vemork, immortalised in the film *The Heroes of Telemark,* and we were to be involved with a re-enactment that involved parachuting four men from the back of a Sea King. One of the men was a Royal Marine, and the grandson of one of the men who took part in the actual raid in February 1943. They parachuted in to the same drop zone as their predecessors had done and then skied the same route as the original men. During the original operation it took the group about four weeks to complete the journey across the country, moving at night and covertly to avoid the German troops. Our group took four days to ski the same route, but the conditions were slightly more favourable and no one was going to shoot them if they were seen.

During our time at Gardermoen, Colin Tattersall and I went and did some downhill skiing. I had never done this before and really enjoyed it. On the first day I kept falling on my left hip when I tried to stop, it was a real nuisance and each time I fell over the young Norwegian children sprayed me with snow. By the end of the day though I had hacked it and only fell a couple of times. After that I did both sorts of skiing, cross country for fitness and downhill for real enjoyment. I even learnt to Telemark ski (traditional Norwegian skiing). I really enjoyed skiing each year and later I completed my Alpine Military Ski Instructor course and have taught for eighteen years all over Europe, Scandinavia and the USA.

CHAPTER 7

The exercise in Southern Norway finished towards the end of March and by the 21st I was home again with Cath and the children. Kieran was now 6 and Simon 4, so both were at school in Queen Camel.

During the few months after Easter leave we were involved in a series of exercises and deployments on board and with the SBS in Scotland near Faslane. On 17 May a day of fighter evasion training sorties had been planned, which involved Hawk fighter jets trying to attack us during a navigation exercise and us trying to avoid them without being shot down; it was the first time I had carried out this type of sortie since the Falklands War. The day was fine, and the Hawk fighter jets performed well. It did make me think back to the Falklands, though these aircraft were only going to shoot us with cameras, not high explosive 20mm cannon shells. Not quite the same. On 31 May I embarked in HMS *Invincible*, but only for two weeks on an exercise called Rough Diamond. This involved inserting Royal Marines in various locations all around the country and then recovering them some days later.

I was still enjoying front-line service, even though I had been on the squadron for three years now; a normal tour is 2½ years. After summer leave I was due on HMS *Hermes* again, but this would be the ship's last deployment. It was to be sold off to the Indian Navy, who also operated the Sea Harrier from the decks. The trip would leave on 14 September and return around the middle of November. A good deployment really, back to the Mediterranean with visits and exercises in Gibraltar, Malta, Italy, Greece, Turkey and Egypt. We were taking two Sea Kings and 845 would take two Wessex Mk5s.

Leading the detachment was the new boss, Lieutenant Commander Neil McMillan. He was known as 'Black Mac' for some reason, though I don't know why. Every time a fellow squadron aircrew colleague would meet him, he would always put his head towards you and say 'DINK' – it was just his thing. He was a good boss and you always knew where you stood with him; he demanded professionalism and competency and I will take it as a compliment that I flew with him most of the time.

All had been going like clockwork until, in the middle of October, the ship started to sail towards Cyprus for an exercise in Turkey. As we neared Cyprus, the squadron was asked to deliver some equipment to Istanbul. This could be tricky because Greece and Turkey were not on friendly terms; we would have to fly up a corridor about four miles wide between Greek and Turkish airspace. I planned the sortie carefully because accurate navigation would be vital.

We flew north up the corridor and had been airborne for about forty minutes, so about seventy miles from the ship and positioned in the centre of the corridor, flying at 1,000ft, as we had been told. All of a sudden, a Phantom Jet fighter of the Greek Air Force came right over the top of us, missing us by about 100ft. The jet blast and turbulence from the aircraft took all lift from our blades and we started to plummet towards the ground. Bill Sample, who was flying, struggled to regain control of the aircraft, we were kicking from side to side and the tail rotor had no effect. At last Bill managed to put the cyclic stick forward, we got some forward speed and therefore control of the aircraft. I presume we had been caught in some form of Vortex Ring. He recovered the aircraft at 100ft above the water, a close call. We were all fuming; Bill made a call on the international distress frequency but the Phantom did not reply, we then made a complaint to the Turkish and Greek Air Traffic Controls, but they denied all knowledge of the Phantom. We continued to Istanbul, fuelled and then went back to *Hermes*. On landing, the operations officer impounded my navigation chart. Between us being taken out by the Phantom and landing on *Hermes*, an airspace incursion had been reported by the Greek authorities. The incident had escalated and words had taken place between the Greek President and Margret Thatcher. A signal had come to *Hermes* from London to impound my chart. The chart was exact though, and I could prove that we were exactly where we should have been and that we had not strayed into Greek Airspace. I'd had VOR, DME and ADF fixes, with a good navigation plot. Once again, my training had come into good use. The issue was not escalated and we heard nothing more at our level. Maybe the diplomats sorted it out between themselves.

When we eventually got into Turkish waters, the flight of four aircraft was to be positioned ashore and work from a forward refuelling point by the coast, this was to test our forward logistics and capabilities. Publicity was part of the whole exercise and getting the press and media on board enabled us to show them how we conducted ourselves and how we operated. The press were being lifted in one of the Wessex Mk5 of 845 Squadron. POACMN 'Topsy' Turner and I were sitting in front of the FOB tent watching what was going on, when the Wessex with the press came into land. It approached in what almost seemed to be slow motion and both Topsy and I exclaimed, 'He is coming in heavy and downwind!' Not a good thing, if you recall my incident in Norway years before. The incident unfolded gradually, second by second; the aircraft descended too quickly and then lost all lift, the dust flew up and then the dust cleared. There sat

CHAPTER 7

the Wessex half on its side, the right wheel and leg had broken on impact and the rotor had hit the ground. Fortunately, it did not roll over completely, but unfortunately, a press man in the back had come out of his harness and been thrown across the cabin and broken his arm. Thankfully, though much to our surprise, there were no reports of the accident in the press. Not quite the image the Navy had been hoping for.

The engineers secured the aircraft and all was OK. The aircraft was made safe and then we considered how to get it back to *Hermes* to be assessed and repaired. A day later, a plan was formulated. Using our Sea King, we would lift the Wessex back to the ship. The lift would be very heavy for us, so the ship would close into the shore to ensure that the Sea King could complete the task with minimal fuel load on board. The boss and I would lift the Wessex and the AEO (Air Engineering Officer) and MAOT would control the rigging of the helicopter. The engines, rotors and tail pylon had been removed to reduce the weight. There was a rigging scheme for the Wessex, but I don't recall anyone ever flying it below a Sea King before; this was a first. The lift in the end was quite uneventful; the run in to the deck was careful, slow and measured. I brought the Wessex in about 30ft above the deck (I didn't want it to crash a second time...) then we slowly lowered it to the deck, all went well.

After a run ashore in Istanbul, we headed down toward Cyprus; after a stopover in Cyprus, we went on to Alexandria in Egypt for an exercise in the Sahara Dessert. First though there was a task to complete for the intelligence services, who suspected that the Egyptians were buying arms from the Soviets. They thought the docks in Alexandria were receiving these items but could not get in and needed photographs to prove it. The problem was, because we were in Egypt, the authorities insisted we flew with an observer to monitor where the aircraft went and what we did. I had to take some photographs of the dock area, so I recruited some troops to fly with us. I put the observer in a seat at the right-front of the cabin, strapped him in tight and said he could not move from there. Then I positioned three of the troops between him and the back door where I would snap the photographs. The observer was not happy, but tough luck. It worked OK and I managed to gather the info requested, we then carried on to the Sahara and I got the photographs delivered later that afternoon. We camped in the desert for about five days then went back to *Hermes* and had a run ashore in Alexandria. What an awful place, dusty, dirty and busy with traffic going in every direction under no sign of control or rights of way. There was one positive though, the street food was great.

On completion of the desert exercise we returned to the ship. It was coming up to that time of year when the promotion signal was transmitted around the Fleet. CPOACMN Charlie Charlton, who was the senior aircrewman from 845, had previously been at Culdrose and had got promoted after being at the Aircrewman's School as an instructor. He was trying to explain to me that the only way to get your Chief's rate was to be an instructor at the Aircrewman's School in Cornwall. It seemed to be true, as most of the promotions during the previous two years had come from there, but I didn't want to go. A few nights later I got a phone call from the boss who said, 'Chief, get to my cabin now.' I said, 'I am not a Chief yet!' That was when he told me I was on the signal and would be promoted first thing in the new year. Great news! News that I had wanted to hear and this was my first shout at getting promoted – and I wouldn't have to become an instructor at Aircrewman's School.

The last exercise took place in the Eastern Med and the ship set sail for Gibraltar, which would take about three days, then home again. The following day we were in the middle of the Med, just south of Italy, when a call came into the ship. A cargo ship about forty miles away was taking on water and the crew needed rescuing before it sank. We quickly briefed and I picked Lel as the second rear crew member with me. Lel had never done a rescue before, so it was a good experience for him. We arrived over the ship, which was listing about 20 degrees to starboard. The crew made ready to be lifted off, so I put Lel down on the double lift and started to recover them. There were ten crew members and we lifted them all off; Lel had done a good job for his first rescue. Not long after we lifted the last man off, the load of timber on the upper deck of the ship started to shift, within fifteen minutes the ship listed over and started to sink. The crew were dropped off in Italy and we flew back to *Hermes*. A job well done!

In time *Hermes* pulled alongside in Gibraltar, the last run ashore before going home. Two days later we sailed for home, but there was a sting in the tail to come for me. On sailing north from Gibraltar and up to the Bay of Biscay, Lieutenant Trevor Jackson and I were called in by the flight commander, who told us to sit down as he had something to show us. As soon as he said that, I wondered what could be coming next. He showed Trevor and me a signal which had originated from the Commanding Officer of 846, who had flown back from *Hermes* two weeks earlier. It stated that the British forces in Beirut in the Lebanon needed help and that HMS *Fearless* was sailing today to the Eastern Mediterranean. It also directed that Trevor and I would transfer from *Hermes* to *Fearless* at 0400 hrs the following morning when the ships passed each other.

My first thought was that Cath would not be happy with this news, and I hoped someone had explained to her where I was going and why I had to go – especially when there were about another ten aircrewmen sitting in the crew room back at Yeovilton, who had not been away for the last three months. I found out later that the new CPOACMN had visited Cath; he told her I was not coming home, but for security reasons would not tell her where I was heading. She had an idea anyway, because the media had broadcast that the British detachment in Beirut needed support and a British Assault ship was heading to the region. This was confirmed to Cath when one of the crewmen from the *Fearless* detachment phoned her and explained what the programme was.

I hurriedly packed all my kit and civvies, got all my flying clothing together, then drew my SA80 rifle and AR5 gas mask. Trevor and I said all our goodbyes to the rest of the detachment and then tried to get some sleep before making ready at 0300 hrs to transfer to *Fearless* at 0400 hrs.

After arriving on Fearless and getting a couple of hours sleep, I went up to the briefing room to be briefed on what was happening and the future programme. All the detachment aircrew were there also, along with the boss and the CPOACMN, Bob Aiston. It was explained to us that we would be supporting BRITFORLEB (British Forces Lebanon) and would be away till at least Christmas, before being relieved. Later, I cornered the CACMN and asked why I was plucked out of *Hermes* when there were other crewmen back at Yeovilton; he declined to say anything other than 'it was a command decision'. It might have been the boss, though I will never know for sure. Cath and I were not impressed.

On the positive side, it was nearly winter in the UK and it was still nice and warm in the Eastern Med. We were going on operations again and might get some really good flying in. There was a good bunch of Petty Officer Aircrewmen on the trip with me, Colin Tattersall, McR and Tab Hunter and of course the CPOACMN Bob Aiston.

The ship entered the Straits of Gibraltar and we headed east after a quick trip into HMS *Rooke*, the Naval base at the airfield on the rock. Then we headed at speed to Cyprus with a strong sense of déjà vu, having left there only a week or so before. Quite a bit of work took place on the trip east, we painted the Union Flag on the nose and side of the aircraft, got the maps we needed and also trained a couple of the lads to operate a spectrum analyser to detect missiles coming in, then we could use Chaff (a decoy made up of lots of little metallic strips), hopefully to deflect the incoming rockets.

Working up with our weapons was a priority, so we did lots of Cabin Gunnery with the GPMG, which is a 7.62mm machine gun in the back doorway. Another priority was to work the crews up on NVG deck operations, to enable us to do landings at sea and ashore at night with no lights.

On arrival at the coast of Lebanon, we were ready for any incident or operation that came our way. All the briefings had been conducted, intelligence had been gathered and routes in and out of Beirut planned. There was a route down the centre of the city along the 'green line', which was a wadi, a trench that ran north/south from the coast to the base where BRITFORLEB was stationed, which was to the south east of the city. This was not long after the Americans had taken a big loss when one of the hotels they used as Headquarters and barracks had been attacked by a large lorry bomb; everyone knew that there was a real and present threat in the city.

One side of the green line was Christian, the other Muslim. The two sides had been fighting each other for a while and the city was a real war zone, with most buildings destroyed or full of bullet and shell holes. Although the French were also operating in the city, the British were the only unit that both sides trusted (I presume from reputation of operation in the region for many years), and so it was the UK Army vehicles that could go most places, on both sides of the green line. BRITFORLEB Land Rovers were painted with a Union Flag, as we did the same on the helicopters; this was a sign that we could be trusted.

The first time we went into Beirut we came in from the north, entered the wadi and flew south. The aircraft was about 50ft above the base of the wadi, so we were below the level of the roofs of any houses that still remained intact. It was quite disturbing looking up at the aerials and shattered buildings. Again, I thought what a waste war is; it just destroys everything that has been built up and worked for over the years and is an utter waste of life.

While we were positioned off the coast of Cyprus, the American Iowa Class Battleship USS *New Jersey* was stationed between us and the Beirut coast. There had been another bombing and it was broadcast that there would be retaliation from the American forces. The next morning, we had planned a sortie into Beirut and our route would take us near the USS *New Jersey*. Normally that would not be a problem, a call and passage close by was OK. But this time was different. A call came from the battleship not to come closer than three miles, or we would be shot down. Predictably,

74

we obeyed; on passing three miles to the north there was suddenly a huge explosion from the *New Jersey* and a shockwave that nearly knocked us out of the sky. The cruiser had fired a broadside with their 16-inch guns, all twelve of them. The *New Jersey* had been a Second World War cruiser and was still in service; it had been modified, with new weapons and systems so the big guns were more accurate, but when she fired all her twelve 16-inch guns at once it was like something from D-Day in 1944. This was something I had never seen before and I must admit it was quite an impressive show of firepower.

The flying continued, but at least we did get some time off. Every week or so the RAF, based in Cyprus with their Chinook helicopters, would take over and give us a chance to let our hair down. The detachment would disembark in Cyprus to either Dhekelia or Akrotiri, where we would play rugby or tennis and obviously go for a couple of runs ashore. The weather was still good, so we could even top up our suntans. Towards the later part of December, I was told I could go home. Back home for Christmas – that was good news. I had been away now for four months, but I knew I would not be home for long. It meant either going to Norway in January, or back to the Lebanon. It was the latter and I was informed of it before I went on Christmas leave, so at least I could prepare Cath for the news over leave, before having to go back to the Med mid-January 1984. There was something to look forward to before going back to sea after leave though, I had to go and see the Captain of Yeovilton to be promoted Chief Petty Officer. That meant more pay and probably a new job when I eventually got back from the Lebanon.

One thing had changed out in the Med, HMS *Fearless* had returned home and been replaced by RFA *Reliant*. This was a container ship, which had been given what was called by the Americans 'The Arapaho Conversion', where all the containers were removed and replaced by an ad hoc flight deck, plus hangar and maintenance area for the embarked helicopter flight, with the containers re-inserted for offices and accommodation.

I left home again in early January to embark in *Reliant*, which was positioned off the Cyprus coast. I had no idea when I would get home, but I had said to Cath that if I could arrange it and programme permitting, I would attempt to organise a holiday in Cyprus around Easter time for the family.

The first month back was spent travelling in and out of Beirut and Cyprus. On 7 February, however, we were told that the British detachment in Beirut was being withdrawn from the Lebanon to embark with us as a standby force, on two days' notice if required. The next day, BRITFORLEB transited with their vehicles up to a town called Jounieh, a port just to the north of Beirut. The flight prepared to lift the vehicles and troops out of a secured area by the harbour side. All was going well; the Muslim militia who controlled the area said we would have safe passage – we weren't convinced their assurances were reliable! Sure enough, as we were approaching to pick up a Land Rover halfway through the operation, over the noise of the rotors we heard, 'WA Thump, WA Thump'. I had heard that sound before, it was shells coming in and they were getting closer and closer. We were in the hover and couldn't do much other than climb and get out of the area; we climbed and set off for *Reliant*. The British authorities complained and after some negotiating the shelling stopped until we had evacuated the Brit force from the coast. By the end of that day, we had all the troops and vehicles on board RFA *Reliant*.

As soon as we had finished withdrawing the troops our next task was to evacuate the British Embassy staff and their dependants, along with citizens who claimed some form of connection to Britain, the Embassy or a relationship to British citizens from Beirut. The situation in Beirut was obviously worsening and the order to evacuate all the British from the city had been received.

The morning of the 10th dawned and we got airborne again. This time we would go on to the coastal road on the northern side of Beirut city, along a route extending from the green line out to sea. The pickup point was on the coast, just in front of the British Embassy, with the landing site situated between the Muslim enclave on one side of the landing site and the Christian enclave to the west. On this occasion both parties kept their word and did not shell or fire at us, I presume because we were evacuating civilians.

We filled up with passengers each time we landed, people of all creed and colour. There were a lot of Brits and some Lebanese who had a tenuous link to British Embassy staff. I held out my hand to help one lady in, but she was grasping her bag with all her might. The bag opened slightly and I saw it was full of gold and diamonds, probably her worldly goods I thought, but there was a lot of wealth in Lebanon at the time.

After a refuel and another round trip, a young woman came to the doorway holding a wicker basket that was closed at the top. She passed the basket to me and I was about to throw it to Dave, who was at the front of the cabin, when I noticed there was a baby in it. Stopping the throw, I helped the woman in and returned her basket. That was the last time we went into Beirut. We had a couple of weeks off the coast, but the operation had come to an end.

CHAPTER 7

During the previous three weeks I had been ashore and organised an apartment near Limassol in Southern Cyprus. I had also put in for leave and got flights for Cath, Kieran and Simon to come out for two weeks. It was then that the flight commander, Jack Lomas, told us that the ship was heading off home! Thankfully, he gave me permission to stay in Cyprus and have my leave out there with my family, so I went ashore as the ship sailed. It was great to see the family again and the next two weeks were fantastic, the first family holiday we'd had for a long time. Sun and sand, the children loved being abroad visiting a different country and seeing all the ancient sites.

While I was on holiday the squadron phoned and told me about a job that had just been established at the Flight Test Centre at the A&AEE Boscombe Down near Salisbury. They were asking for volunteers to go there. I had been on 846 now for four years, of which three years had been away, either on exercise or operations; this new job would mean a break from going away all the time and a chance to have some home life. I volunteered, and fortunately the person who chose the successful applicant was my old boss from the Falklands War, now Commander Simon Thornewill, the Commanding Officer of D Squadron at Boscombe Down. I know that about eight Chief Aircrewmen had put in for the appointment, but I managed to get the place and would join there in the August of 1984. When the holiday ended I managed to take some extra re-engaging leave which meant I got to spend nearly a month with Cath and the children.

On returning from leave I went back to do my leaving routine and to say goodbye to everyone. It was about midday and I was about to leave, when the Chief Aircrewman said, 'Where are you going? I have not said you could go.' I was a Chief who had been on the squadron for four years, plus it was Friday afternoon and I was going on draft. You can imagine what I had to say to that – it was not pleasant. He said nothing to me when I turned my back on him, walked out of the door and finally left.

I wasn't joining Boscombe Down until August, so I instructed on 707 Squadron for six weeks. Alf Tupper was the Warrant Officer Aircrewman there and it was good to renew our old working relationship.

Chapter 8

I arrived at Boscombe Down in August and it was a bit of a culture shock. The establishment was A&AEE which meant Aircraft and Armament Experimental Establishment and was mainly run by an MOD department called the Procurement Executive (MODPE). I joined D squadron, which later became Rotary Wing Test Squadron (RWTS), it was a tri-service unit with pilots drawn from the RAF, Army and RN, plus an exchange pilot from Canada. All these pilots had completed the Empire Test Pilots' course, either in the US, France, or the UK at ETPS – the Empire Test Pilots' School.

Up until then there had been only one RAF Loadmaster on the staff, but I was about to double the complement by being the first permanent Naval aircrewman to join the squadron.

The task of the unit was to test and evaluate any new aircraft or equipment fitted to aircraft of all three Services. To that end, we would fly in all military helicopter types that the MOD owned plus, now and then, other aircraft that might need testing.

As I needed to be qualified on all these aircraft, I had to go on a couple of courses. The first was the Chinook course at RAF Odiham. The aircraft was superb, capable and quite complicated to operate, but a joy to fly in. I completed the course, with a pass and then returned to D Squadron to get into the trials' flying. The flying was pretty wide and varied; I would fly in all sorts of helicopters from Scout and Gazelle to Sea King, Puma and Chinook. We would test the aircraft systems, flight profiles, armaments, radios, engines, icing capabilities and emergencies.

The role of the aircrewman on the squadron was to fly periodically in the left-hand seat of some of the helicopters. I was already quite a handy pilot from my time on 846, but the variety of aircraft on D Squadron was a challenge. There was a Scout, a small AAC version of the Naval Wasp, single engine, no flight computer or automatic stabilisation system (autopilot). The first time I flew the Scout it was a real seat-of-the-pants experience and I vowed to get the hang of it ASAP. The Scout had hydraulic assistance for the controls, but could be flown without hydraulics and that was my ambition, to fly and land the Scout without hydraulic assistance. I managed it after two hours flying and was really chuffed with myself, proving I could achieve it.

Some flight trials in the Chinook consisted of climbing to 15,000ft; we would wear parachutes and have oxygen, in case of an emergency at altitude. When we had climbed to height we shut down one of the two engines and then carried out tests on the remaining engine for power and icing capabilities.

Another flight was to help the students of the Empire Test Pilots' School course to carry out a height climb. This was in a Gazelle, a light, single engine helicopter, again oxygen was used and we wore parachutes as we climbed to 20,000ft above Boscombe Down. I noted all the details of engine and speed performance as we climbed and eventually achieved 20,000ft; we actually got to 20,059ft before maxing out. It's a long way up in a very small aircraft, but over Boscombe Down the weather was gin clear and I could see the north coast of France.

I had thought going to D Squadron meant there would be no more going away for a while, but in January 1985 the Chinook had to carry out an icing trial. Not really viable in the UK, so it would happen at the Royal Canadian Air Force Base Shearwater, near Halifax in Nova Scotia. The weather there is wet and cold, perfect for icing at altitude. The trial was run by a combined team from Boeing and MOD PE, with military test aircrew and civilian test engineers. The trial was all about getting icing clearance for the Chinook and examine the amount of ice accretion (build up), mainly on the twin main rotor heads and blades. The blades had inbuilt heaters in the leading edges and if icing occurred the heaters would switch on and de-ice the blades in flight.

I had to go away again, but only for three months – and this time living in an apartment and getting well paid for it. The trial was carried out mainly at altitude, and on one flight we had a serious problem with the electrics, with the radios and navigation aids failing. We were up at 10,000ft and in cloud, the only option was to go down to what is called 'safety altitude' (where you won't hit anything), this we did but the aircraft was still in cloud. We had an idea of our position, but not to a pinpoint and could not get down without radio communications with Shearwater. Our options were to try and navigate over Shearwater and see if there was a gap to get down, or take the Chinook out to sea and abandon it, (i.e. jump out of the aircraft and let it crash into the sea).

The pilots and I discussed the options and I communicated the plan to the six test observers in the back of the aircraft. I explained to them that I would lower the ramp at the back of the aircraft and bring them forward one at a time, then they would jump clear, pull the ripcord and hopefully we would all join up on the surface. They all looked at me stunned and asked if I was joking; I said that I wasn't, and if we couldn't get down to land at Shearwater, we would have to jump so they should get prepared. Fortunately for all of us, as we came over the top of Shearwater there was a break in the cloud, and we dived down and recovered to the airfield. Back on terra firma! Thank goodness.

The trial proved that the de-icing system on the Chinook worked, but the amount of power required was immense and a third generator needed to be fitted. That was one of the main findings and a problem for us, as our trials' aircraft had only two generators fitted, which had been one of the reasons for our electrical failure earlier in the trial. All the data gathered was then shared and published. Eventually, it was decided that the British military would not buy the de-icing system, although all the data did come in to play for later projects on other aircraft de-icing systems.

After ten weeks in Canada, we had to deliver the Chinook back to the Boeing plant near Philadelphia. I planned the flight; we would leave Shearwater, fly down the east coast into America, down to Boston where we would refuel and then through New York airspace down to Wilmington, near Philadelphia. There we would spend another two weeks flying and report writing before going home via Washington.

On return to D Squadron, the boss told us that a change had happened and the squadron was to be renamed RWTS (Rotary Wing Test Squadron). I'm not sure why the name was changed, but at least it did say we were a test squadron, and also stopped any confusion with D Squadron SAS, I think.

The remainder of the year involved a lot of trials in various aircraft, from performance testing to heavy lift in the Chinook, weapons trials in the Sea King Mk2/5 ASW aircraft. Torpedo drops and missile recovery in the Wessex took place at the range in Benbecula, which is in the north west of Scotland.

I now had nearly 4,000 hours flying in many different types of helicopters. The job was good, and the guys I worked with were a tremendous bunch of people.

The boss called me in one day and presented me with a bar to go on the GSM I received for NI, the bar was for the Lebanon Operation in 1983/4. He also gave me my LSGC (Long Service and Good Conduct Medal); this was for fifteen years good conduct and service after the age of 17½. Most people call it a medal for fifteen years of undetected crime; I might not fully justify that remark as I had not been a good boy all the time, but now I had three medals and a bar to one of them, a veritable chest full.

In November 1985 the boss called me in again. The RN had decided to purchase an upgrade to the ASW Sea King Mk5 to Mk6. This would be a modification programme where Mk5s would be modified to Mk6s, with a modern Active and Passive SONAR system. To that end, I would have to go and complete the ASW (Anti-Submarine Warfare) course at RNAS Culdrose in Cornwall.

I would be at home for Christmas leave, then down to Cornwall to start the course, which would last until the end of October. Two benefits did come out of doing the course though. The flying pay was better if you had an ASW qualification, and there had been a change in the promotion qualifications in the Aircrewman Branch which meant aircrewmen needed an ASW tick in the box for future advancement. Yes, I could one day be promoted to Warrant Officer if I qualified. Becoming a Warrant Officer was one of my ambitions, along with becoming a Standards Examiner (trapper) on Naval Flying Standards. I would achieve both in due course.

The first phase of the course covered Active SONAR and lasted till the end of February; it involved learning how active SONAR (pinging) worked and how to use the equipment and employ the best tactics to find and destroy enemy submarines. The next phase was classroom based and was to learn about passive SONAR; how to utilise the information extracted from the displays on the passive SONAR display and employ tactics using the passive SONAR to track and eventually destroy a submarine. Along with this was oceanography, which is basically underwater meteorology, studying currents and how sound travels through water at different depths and temperatures. The third part of the course covered airborne passive SONAR operations, with a final check ride including both active and passive sonar and a submarine exercise. Finally, at the end of October the course concluded. I had achieved a first-class pass both on the ground and in the air; I was pleased with the results and happy that I could get home again each night, rather than just at the weekends.

At the beginning of 1987 there was a deck trial to clear the Chinook landing scheme for HMS *Intrepid/Fearless* (old ships), this lasted a week and it was nice to see the Death Star (nickname for *Intrepid*) again. Lieutenant Al Howden and I visited Westland's of Yeovil to assess the cockpit and rear workstations of a future helicopter that was in development.

This was an ASW aircraft and was known then as the EH101; it would later be developed and become the Merlin. More deck trials and weapon trials continued throughout the year.

A highlight of the year was to fly a series of trials, with the new boss, Lieutenant Colonel Wally Steward AAC, in the A109s which we had brought back from the Falklands. They had both been given to the SAS air squadron at Hereford. The trial consisted of high-speed runs with weapons and tactical entry equipment, fast roping and parachuting.

The opportunity also came around to carry out another parachute jump. The Chinook was going to be used for the Empire Test Pilots' course annual parachute jump. The other RWTS crewman, Master Aircrew Pete Simmons, would act as the loadmaster for the sortie, so I could also do the jump. ETPS carried out this water jump into the bay off Studland just south of Poole in Dorset to give confidence to the students if they ever had to abandon an aircraft over the sea.

It had been a great year for a steady home life; I had only been away for about four weeks and I had the chance to be with Cath and the children. Kieran was now 11 and attended boarding school in Wellington, Somerset. Simon was 9 and would follow Kieran to Wellington School when he was 10.

During the summer of 1988, I was informed that I would be leaving RWTS and going down to RNAS Culdrose in October of that year to become the CPOACMN of 826 Squadron. This was an ASW unit that mainly operated on Royal Fleet Auxiliary ships, frigates or smaller craft in single aircraft detachments or flights.

During my tour at Boscombe Down, I also took the opportunity to do some fixed-wing flying. I had flown in a Hunter and Jet Provost previously, but no modern jets. So when the Fast Jet Test Squadron asked if we would like to go up, I jumped at the chance. First, I had to do all the extra drills, which included ejection seat emergencies and abandon aircraft procedures. I had already carried out the hypoxia and parachute drills for our RWTS trials.

The next day I went up in the Hawk, the experience was exhilarating, flying – but a different experience from my normal helicopter flying. A week later I flew in the Harvard, an old Second World War aircraft, which Boscombe used for photographic chase. I had a chance to fly both aircraft and I must say, they were quite easy to fly compared to a helicopter. One of my last flights at Boscombe was in a Hawk with the Air Commodore of A&AEE and he asked where I would like to go. Because of my move to

CHAPTER 8

Cornwall, I was looking at buying a house in Godolphin Cross, near RNAS Culdrose, so, I asked if we could go there. The weather was OK as we got down to Culdrose, we carried out a ground-controlled approach to the main runway. Our new house was on the extended centre line of the runway, so when we overshot the approach the pilot flipped the Hawk upside down, we were looking down on to my house. I pointed it out, and then we turned the right way up and went back to Boscombe via the south coast. I flew the aircraft back and landed it; that was the last time I flew a fixed-wing for quite a few years.

The job at RWTS had been so different from a Naval squadron; sometimes the flying had been at the forefront of aviation, while other flights were long and arduous, but maybe a little tedious, flights like radio and inertia navigation trials. Having had the opportunity to fly in so many different types of helicopter, twenty in total, in so many varying environments and in so many different roles was a real experience and enhancement to my career. The experience and level of aviation knowledge I had gained over the past four years was incredible.

The boss Wally Steward and I had flown together quite often, so he knew how competent I was as a pilot. He wanted me to transfer as a pilot to the Army Air Corps (AAC). The AAC still let non-commissioned officers fly as pilots. He approached them, but they stated that unfortunately I was too senior to transfer. So that was the end of that; it was a challenge that I would have enjoyed taking on.

Chapter 9

It was now September 1988 and after four years at Boscombe Down, it was time to return to Naval Service with 826 Squadron. First, I had to do a refresher course on 706 Squadron to make sure my ASW skills were still up to speed, then I joined my new squadron halfway through October.

First thing to do was to settle in, both at home and on 826 Squadron. Cath was OK at home; it was a new house and we had been living there for two months. Kieran and Simon were both at Wellington Boarding School and Cath found a part-time job at a place called GMS in St Erth, near Camborne. She was a vegetable trimmer, but I said she was a Vegetable Technician, which sounded better! In October my father became very ill while I was on detachment in Benbecula in the Outer Hebrides, he had been ill with a form of blood cancer for some time. I was quickly flown back to RNAS Culdrose, collected my car and, with Cath, drove up to Nottingham where my parents lived. By the time we got to Nottingham my father had died; it is sad to say, but I didn't shed a tear for him as there was very little love between us. He had shown little interest in me as a child growing up, and also my career in the military.

Fitting in on 826 was my problem though, I had never served on an ASW Squadron before. Yes, I was qualified to do the job, but I didn't have any front-line experience or the street cred and I was the Chief Aircrewman; the man in charge of the aircrewmen on the squadron. To that end, I grabbed a couple of the more experienced ASW crewmen and told them to teach me all they knew; make me a complete operator and teach me everything that was required of an ASW operator and get me the street cred I sorely needed, so that nobody could accuse me of not knowing what I was talking about. I gained the knowledge and experience in double time and within two months I had achieved my aim.

My Commanding Officer on 826 was Lieutenant Commander Phil Shaw, a very experienced Sea King operator, whose reputation went before him.

CHAPTER 9

My Exec Officer (XO) was Lieutenant Commander Bill Harper and he was my reporting officer; he was also a really nice man. I had made changes to the way the crewmen were organised and led on the unit by putting a Petty Officer in charge of each of the four operational flights while I was the CPO in the HQ; I would go away with each flight in turn, to operate, work with and get to know my crewmen. The change worked; the boss and XO thought that the crewmen on the squadron were doing a fantastic job.

While I had been serving at Boscombe Down, the Navy had introduced an instructor course and qualification for aircrewmen. Even though I had instructed previously for about six years, I was now not qualified so the boss suggested I do the instructor's course. It was two weeks long, with a week instructional technique phase and based at Culdrose, so no travelling issues as I could do the course while living at home. On completion of the course, I achieved a good pass and all the students were given a B2 category instructors qualification. On return to the squadron and carrying out a test ride with the Senior Observer, I gained my 'Competence to Instruct' certificate in the ASW role. The next step was to be upgraded to B1 category, and to achieve that you needed a certain amount of instructional flying hours and a ground/air examination by Royal Naval Standard Flight (NFSF) (or 'Trappers' as they are known). After a short while I had achieved the required instructional hours and knowledge in the ASW role and was trapped by WOACMN 'Bomber' Mills of the NFSF. Bomber had been on my PO qualifying course, so I knew him well and the trap went well, but still not a breeze. I had done my homework though and achieved a good pass.

As part of our continuation training as aircrew, we were encouraged to attend the RAF Winter Survival Course, held in Bad Kohlbrug in Southern Germany, near Munich. I volunteered and got a place on the course which lasted two weeks and involved some ground navigation exercises, escape and evasion and best of all, some downhill skiing instruction. I flew out from Heathrow to Munich and made my way with a few other students to Bad K. As usual for the RAF, the accommodation was in a nice hotel. After settling in we met the other students, who were from all three Services. I was teamed up with Dave, a Staff Sergeant from the Army Air Corps. We went out and did our navigation exercise during the day and then at night we carried out another navigation task. My partner was not great at navigation, so I took the lead and we made our points after a bit of debate, I am sure he didn't trust a matelot at navigation! After arriving at one side of a wood, Dave said we were in the wrong place, I said if we went straight through the wood, our rendezvous (RV) point was on the other side. I assured him I was correct (hoping I was of course). When we emerged on the far side of the trees, there was our RV, to my relief.

The next day was a survival exercise, where we had to build a shelter and stay out for the night. After Norway this was as easy as pie. The basher (a quickly constructed shelter) was up in an hour or so, with a fire going and we settled in for the night.

On returning to the hotel, we were told that the skiing phase would start the next day; I was happy with that. We had an Austrian ski instructor and were going up to the Zugspitze, a 10,000ft mountain with a glacier on top. The instruction was great, and I progressed quickly. This was the first real ski instruction I had ever had, and it was to set the future tone for my alpine skiing during the rest of my career.

After the skiing phase, there came some more navigation followed by some escape and evasion instruction, plus techniques like river crossing. The river we had to cross still had ice flowing down it and the technique was to undress and put your clothes into a Gortex bivouac bag. The options were to get naked or to keep your knickers on; the Navy and the Army got naked, but the RAF kept their underpants on, funny old things. With the dry clothes in the Bivouac bag, the trick was to get as much air into the bag as you could then tie the end so it acted as a float. We then had to get into the water and swim across the river. The water was flipping freezing, and I'm not kidding when I say ice bergs were flowing past me. When we got to the other side, I managed to climb out, just! I think I had turned into a girl though, as my bits were now inverted with the cold and my gonads had almost disappeared into my stomach. I dried myself off as best as I could then dressed, at least I had dry underpants to put back on after the crossing.

The next phase was the Escape and Evasion (E&E), I was still paired up with Dave the Army Staff Sergeant. Over the next few days a company of German Army ski troops would be looking for us; we would travel at night and sleep during the day – well that was the plan. One problem though, the troops had NVG and thermal images to see us at night, so we would really stand out if we weren't careful.

We had been given some white parachute material as camouflage so Dave and I manufactured a camouflage suit each, they were pretty good really.

We set off and made the first check point and met up with our contact agent, who gave us the next RV, which was on the other side of a large forest in the middle of Bavaria. About an hour later I heard the sound of skis

Above left: Me joining the Royal Navy at HMS *Raleigh*, September 1968.

Above right: Cath and me getting married at St Josephs Church, Adlington, on 12 April 1971.

Before and after ten days' survival training in the New Forest, November 1972.

Me, Joe 'Derby' Allen and 'Slim' Freelove at the start of OFT on 707 Squadron, 1973.

Above left: Wessex Mk5 after double engine flame out, Norway, 1974.

Above right: My first parachute jump at Bridlington in the summer of 1976.

RNAS Yeovilton Junglie Aircrewmen on Air Day just before the Commando Assault.

Us playing rugby against the USMC at Camp Lejeune.

Two 845 Wessex Mk5s on the Glacier in South Georgia.

Above left: HMS *Antelope* exploding.

Above right: HMS *Antelope* breaking up in San Carlos Water and sinking.

Two Sea Kings Mk4s of 846 squadron over HMS *Coventry* ten miles north of West Falkland.

Above left: Over HMS *Coventry*, in total more than twelve helicopters and boats from HMS *Broadsword* rescued most of the crew in less than two hours.

Above right: A fragment of the bomb which blew up our tent at the FOB site on the side of San Carlos Water, 31 May 1982.

Sir *Galahad* at Bluff Cove.

VA (ZA298) in Impassable Valley after being hit by 20mm cannon shell, with Paul Massey on the rotor head while changing the damaged blade.

Section of the damaged blade now in the FAA Museum.

846 Squadron detachment coming home on HMS *Fearless*, 1982.

Above left: Cath, Kieran and Simon with me on my homecoming from the Falklands, 1982. In the background is the Captured A109 that Pete Rainey and I flew back from HMS *Fearless*.

Above right: Kieran and Simon doing some flag waving.

Alf Tupper and me in front of VA, August 1982.

The Squadron personnel after the run from King Alfred's Tower.

Above left: Lifting a Wessex Mk5 of 845 Squadron back on board HMS *Hermes*, 1983.

Above right: Delta submarine north of Russian coast

Chinook Mk1
Icing Trial in
Canada, 1985.

848 Squadron Aircrewmen in Al Jubail during the First Gulf War, January 1991.

11am in the desert west of KKMC when the Kuwait Oil fields were burning.

Flying into downtown Sarajevo, 1993.

Us lifting stores and a Sea Harrier Engine to HMS *Illustrious* off the Sierra Leone coast.

Above left: Gun and one tonne vehicle lift from HMS *Ocean*.

Above right: Achieving my 7,000 flying hours in Afghanistan, 2002.

Final Flight in Afghanistan, 2002.

Me flying the Apache with Tim Peake over Boscombe Down.

Above left: The statue of Mother Russia near Volgograd, note the people to the left of the statue.

Above right: Nolan and me after our soaking.

8,000 flying hours and another good soaking.

Forty years of military aviation.

The picture showing all the types of helicopter I have flown in during my flying career in the RN and RAF.

whooshing along the snow, I told Dave to run like hell and get some cover. Fortunately for me I was quite fit and was faster than Dave; unfortunately for him, he fell. I didn't want to shout, so I helped him up and set off again. He fell a second time and this time I saw the troops coming after us. That was it; self-preservation took hold and I scarpered as fast as I could. Dave unfortunately got caught, but that's life.

I was now on my own in the middle of the Bavarian forest, it was about 2am, dark as hell and there were 200 ski troops out there, waiting for escapees like me to make a mistake. I started out again after laying up for about an hour waiting until the German troops had disappeared. I set out for the next RV and had walked about another mile when I heard voices; I dived into the snow and kept perfectly still. The voices got louder and louder, the speech was English, I looked up and could just make out the silhouette of two men coming towards me. They were two British RAF Airmen (I thought this is like something out of the TV comedy *'Allo 'Allo*. I relaxed and waited until they were right on top of me, they hadn't seen me due to my white camouflage against the snow. All of a sudden, I stood up and said 'Hello'. They nearly jumped out of their skins. After they had calmed down, I told them what had happened and to take care and to talk a little quieter as I had heard them from quite a distance away. After the conversation we split up and went our separate ways, there was no way I was staying with them; a singleton was a much more difficult target to catch and I figured my chances were better on my own.

The briefing at the start of the exercise was that if you became separated, you were to make the next RV and would be teamed up with another runner. I made the next RV, waited the prerequisite period while watching the agent, and then made contact.

Unfortunately, the exercise rules had been changed by the staff and as I made contact, six German troops came out and captured me. The staff had decided that everyone would be captured, so that was that: a prisoner of war (not quite the same as the Falklands though, I thought). All the PoWs were now shipped to the interrogation facility, I was stripped and given my boots back, without laces, and a pair of overalls.

Next, we were all marched around a field, it was about -2°C outside, and I was shivering when we finally got into the centre itself. I thought this was a bit better, at least it was warmer; what a fool I was! During the next twenty-four hours we were put in the stress position and bombarded with either white noise or being interrogated. The interrogation phases were a welcome break from the stress positions and white noise.

The second session of interrogation was by the female/male combination. We had all been briefed on this type of technique. The woman would make you strip off and then she would take the micky out of the size of your manhood (it was still cold and shrunken), and then the man would have a go at trying to wind you up. This lasted about half an hour, but then it was back to the stress position. You lost track of time and with no sleep you were exhausted after the evasion phase and the stress of the whole exercise.

The last interrogation was conducted by a single man. He started off really nice, gave me a cup of tea and a biscuit (always accept food and drink I had been told). I was halfway through my tea, when he said that if I didn't talk it would be very bad for me. I answered with my Name, Rank, Number and date of birth. He didn't see the good side of that, he smashed the teacup out of my hand and said I would be taken out and shot, this was my last chance. I made the same reply. At that, two of the prisoner handlers came in, whisked me up and out of the room, to an area outside where a firing squad was waiting. They positioned me against a wall and covered my head with a sack. The interrogator asked again and I replied, with the same answer. He ordered that I should be shot. The firing squad then cocked their weapons.

The next moment I was shuffled away to a nice warm room. The exercise was over, and I had managed to survive without talking or caving in to the interrogation. After a good night's sleep, I was rewarded with another two days' skiing and then it was time to go home. This was a survival exercise that taught you a lot about yourself and how you would react in a very stressful situation.

A week later I was travelling to work along the main road from Camborne to Helston, when all of a sudden, a car started to pull out from a side road on my left. I was doing about 55 mph and there was nothing I could do about it; I was going to hit the car. The woman driving the car had pulled out so late, that if I didn't steer to the right, my front-right wing would go straight into the driver's door of her car. If that happened, I would kill her, so I made the conscious decision to hit the engine bay of her car with the front of my car. My car was a Vauxhall Cavalier, quite a sturdy car and it would hopefully take the hit. I hit her front end, my car swung round and ended up facing halfway across the road; hers had done almost a 360-degree turnaround. I was shaken but OK, so I got out and checked how the woman was. She was still in the car, but looked to be not badly injured. Her door was jammed, but I managed to prise it open and as she got out she was crying, extremely shaken and said that her foot had slipped off the clutch, which was why she had pulled out in front of me. When the police arrived, the constable asked

CHAPTER 9

if I was OK, and if I was, could I direct the traffic. I then said the woman had admitted to me that her foot had slipped on the clutch and that was why she had pulled out in front of me. I managed to get all my insurance back and buy another Cavalier, but it was another close call between life and death (another life gone).

The men on the 826 squadron were a good bunch and I enjoyed my time there. The flying was varied and sometimes demanding because the squadron was split into flights, which had different tasks and roles to undertake. It made for some extraordinary tasking at times. On one trip we went up to Norway and the boss and I taught the crews to mountain fly, which was an eye-opener for some of the less experienced crewmen and pilots, as they had never been taught the procedures and techniques for approaches and landing in the mountains, let alone to the top of 10,000ft peaks and ridges covered in snow.

The most demanding detachment though, was in the summer of 1989, for eight weeks around the north coast of Norway and Russia. It was from the beginning of May till the end of July, which meant the sun didn't set the whole trip; that does things to your mindset and upsets the body clock. The detachment which took place about twenty miles off the coast of Russia consisted of testing a new SONAR array that would eventually go into the new Merlin Helicopter. We were in the hover, or dip as it is called, at about 40ft above the water, I had lowered the array to about 60ft below the water and started the test. As the sortie progressed, the pilots could see a submarine coming towards us on the surface. I called the contact and both the observer and pilot confirmed they agreed it was the same submarine; the boat continued on the surface tracking to the left of us, when all of a sudden, the Russian Delta Class submarine turned towards us and sped up. The pilots shouted: 'The contact is coming straight for us.' They had turned and either were going to take us out, or try to get us to cut the cable on the SONAR. Then Stan, the pilot, said in a very urgent voice, 'John, get the sonar body up quick.'

I had to fold the array first, before we could recover the body. The Delta was bearing down on us, but I had to wait for a green light, to show me the array had completed its folding sequence, Stan was now shouting for me to hurry. At last, the green light came on. I told Stan and we started what is called a 'free stream recovery', that means just pull in power, climb and get the 100ft of cable and array out of the water ASAP. As we started to climb, the observer pulled the blind down from his window. We could see the conning tower of the Delta about 30 yards away, heading directly at us.

The array came out of the water like a rocket and I proceeded to recover the cable and array while we went into a slow forward climb. It had been a close call; I'm sure the submarine would have hit us if we hadn't climbed, but we'll never know for sure.

I thought that was the excitement over for the time being, but the next day we were near the international coastal limit, about thirteen miles off the Russian coast; we were in the hover again, but this time there was no submarine. We had been in the hover for about ten minutes when we received a radio call from our ship that a fast-moving jet was coming our way. Our hover height was 40ft over the water. Stan, who was flying again, spotted the jet – it was coming straight for us at about 150ft. This was shades of the incident off the coast of Turkey a few years before. The jet, a Mig 25 of the Russian Air Force, came directly over us; the jet wash nearly knocked us out of the sky, but Stan managed to gain control very quickly, at least this time we had seen the aircraft coming, unlike the incident in the Mediterranean.

After returning from the North Sea and going back to Culdrose, I found the squadron was still running well. New crewmen came in and those who had done their time on the squadron left, but the new system was working OK. I like to think that I was doing a fair job. It came to write-up time, I'd had been a CPOACMN for some five years, but promotion was a bit static. The structure of the branch meant that the six Warrant Officer jobs were filled, and by relatively young men. This was called 'dead man's shoes' promotion (i.e. someone had to die, leave the service or get into trouble and lose his rank, before anyone else could get a shout at advancement). Even so, we all wanted to get a good report; the officer who was to be my first reporting officer was Bill Harper, my second reporter was the boss, Phil Shaw. We all got on really well and when my report had been completed I was called in to see Bill to get the breakdown. The first thing he said was: 'How do you do it?' He explained that I had got an incredible write up from the boss and he had given me 'walk on water points' (meaning only Jesus might have got a report like that).

The boss wanted me to go to Naval Flying Standards Flight as the trapper when I left 826. I was prepared for that, as Phil Shaw had mentioned it to me previously. I was now a fully qualified and experienced ASW operator, having done a tour as a Test flight Aircrewman at Boscombe Down, and I was SAR qualified, but still my heart was in commando flying. Towards the end of 1990 Saddam Hussein decided to do a bit of force projection and invade Kuwait and the Commando Helicopter Force (CHF) at Yeovilton made contingency plans for going to the Middle East. The squadrons were short of a suitably qualified Chief Aircrewman and apparently I was the only one who could fill the slot; the drafting officer called me to say that I would be posted back to 845 Squadron at Yeovilton in a week's time. The boss got the same call about my move, from the commander in charge of the CHF. All was sorted.

I was in two minds; Cath and I had moved and bought a house in Cornwall, but we had much preferred living in Somerset. I was happier being a commando aircrewman, but I had no choice in the move anyway as I had been ordered to go (life in a blue suit, they say). When I told Cath she was a little disgruntled, but not too much. We decided that we would try to sell our house in Cornwall, or at least rent it out and move to a married quarter in Yeovil for the time being.

Chapter 10

I packed all my gear (again!) and said goodbye to the men on 826 Squadron; I did a very quick handover to Chief Aircrewman Matt Mathews, who would take over from me as the 826 CPOACMN and was due to arrive from NFSF a couple of weeks after I had departed.

I drove up to Yeovilton the following Sunday to join 707 Squadron and carried out a week of refresher flying in the commando role. It had been seven years since I had last flown in the Sea King Mk4 operationally.

Cath came up to Yeovil two weeks later and we moved into a married quarter at Fairmead Road on the outskirts of Yeovil. To say that the quarter was a disappointment was an understatement, it was like something out of the 1950s and Cath was not a happy person. It took a lot of work to get it up to our standard when we eventually moved in

Not long after I moved I was involved in an incident that nearly snookered all my plans. I was playing squash with another crewman called Brian Johnson, when he smashed the ball into my eye. I knew instantly that I had a haemorrhage in my eye, as blood filled my eyeball. I had experienced this before when playing rugby. Brian took me to the sickbay; the medics then drove me to the eye hospital in Taunton. I was on my back for a week, but recovered a short while later. Since then I have always worn squash safety glasses – I had learnt that lesson the hard way.

While I was away in hospital things had changed with my appointment and future position on 845. At the time there were only two front-line commando squadrons, 845 and 846. Their Lordships in the Admiralty had decided that three front-line units would give them greater scope during what was to become the First Gulf War; 848 Squadron was about to form, I would be the CPOACMN with Lieutenant Commander Nigel North as the CO and Lieutenant Commander J.F.R. Evans as the Senior Pilot. The aircrew and engineers would come from all around the Fleet Air Arm; 845, 846 and 707 would supply the aircraft and some personnel. The three front-line units would then have six Sea King Mk4 helicopters each, 845 and 848 would be going to the deserts of Saudi Arabia on 2 January 1991, to deploy before the start of the First Gulf War. 846 would sail to the Gulf aboard RFA *Argus*, which had been converted to a hospital ship for the period of the operation.

I managed to recruit a motley bunch of crewmen, some from 845 and 846, with others from 707 Squadron and some brought back from other units and military establishments. One crewman was Sergeant 'Wombat' Wooldridge, whom I taught on 707 when I left 846 in 1984, he had been moved back to the Royal Marine Corps to 40 Commando at Taunton. The RSM said he couldn't go, but I think I had more power on my side and the drafter made the decision that I would have Wombat on my crew. I don't think the RSM was too pleased.

I knew all the aircrewmen I had recruited from the past; most I had worked with before and knew they had kept their noses clean, worked hard and did a good job. There were a few, however, with whom I had crossed paths and had an issue with their work ethic. I got them together and explained that we were going to war. I said, 'I know you and you know me, now let's make a fresh start and we'll have a great relationship, but if you rot me up, I will come down on you like a ton of bricks.' They understood exactly where I was coming from. The squadron formed and we worked up for the Gulf War, after that we flew the aircraft onto the new *Atlantic Conveyor* (the old one was lost in the Falklands war, sunk by an Exocet missile); we would meet the aircraft again after Christmas in Al Jubail, a port on the coast of Saudi Arabia.

Christmas with the family was great, but there was an underlying tension. Cath was more worried about me going to the Gulf than any other conflict I had been previously involved in. Saddam Hussein had used chemical weapons and that frightened her more than anything. We had worked up with all the chemical and biological training that was required and I told her not to worry, but that was easy for me to say.

On New Year's Day, Cath and the boys drove me into Yeovilton to get the coach that would take us to Brize Norton and then on to the Gulf and Al Jubail. She had a tear in her eye, but at least she had Kieran and Simon with her this time, and lots of friends in Yeovil to take her mind off what I would be doing for the foreseeable future.

We flew out of Brize Norton and arrived in Saudi Arabia, then everyone made their way to The Ressiat, which was a British workers' residence on the outskirts of Al Jubail. We had to sleep four to a room on bunk beds, but the food was pretty good and it was better than living in the field.

The air battle hadn't started yet, but we all made ready because when it did start, we all expected retaliation in the form of Scud missiles from the Iraqi forces and that these would probably be filled with some form of chemicals.

Eventually the ship arrived in Al Jubail, with our aircraft embarked. We flew the helicopters to the harbourside and set up an operating base inside the dockyard, where it was secure from outside sources.

On the passage to the Gulf the maintainers had modified the aircraft with a new GPS system that allowed us to pinpoint our position within metres anywhere in the world. Trouble was no one knew how to use it! I was tasked to go to the RAF Puma squadron which had been deployed to the Gulf before Christmas and learn how the TANS 252 GPS system worked and try to understand its operating procedures. On arrival at the Puma base I was met by one of their senior navigators, given a five-minute lesson on the system and its operating procedures and then went for a half-hour flight to see the TANS 252 in action. It worked well, and after half-an-hour's experience I was the squadron 'expert' and had to teach the rest of the aircrew on 848 how to use it. It was like the blind leading the blind. However, I soon got the hang of things and eventually became an actual expert on the system.

We learnt how to operate much better in the desert than we had previously, the aircraft had sand particle filters fitted to protect the engines and all the compartments were sealed against sand infiltration. The machine guns were covered in parachute material and cleaned using as little oil as possible, to avoid sand getting into the working parts. Then, on 17 January, the air war started; that night we expected retaliation and early the next morning the first Scuds started arriving in Saudi Arabia, some around Al Jubail, but not too close. By then we had learnt to get dressed in our nuclear, biological and chemical (NBC) suits within minutes, and because the air raids lasted hours we eventually managed to get some sleep in our gas masks, but it wasn't comfortable at all and some people still managed to snore in them.

We had now named the Sea King Mk4 forward operating base (FOB) at Al Jubail RNAS 'Banana Split', which was Nigel North's idea – I have no idea why but he was the boss! The area was secure but I knew we didn't have long there before we left. The boss had briefed us that a few days later we would move closer to the Iraqi border and start living in the desert and operating out of the forward operating area close to KKMC (King Khalid Military City). It was on 23 January the squadron upped sticks, flew along the main supply route (MSR) and set up camp about twenty miles south-east of KKMC, close to the Iraqi/Saudi border. While we were there we did a lot of training including a great deal of medevac sorties. We now had RAF paramedics attached to each helicopter crew and they were employed mainly on accidents down the main supply route from KKMC to the coast where the driving was really hazardous.

There were continual Scud alerts, so everyone dug huge shell scrapes and covered them with KIP sheets (8ft square waterproof sheeting). They worked really well to keep the rain and sand out.

We settled into the FOB and tried to make ourselves as comfortable as possible. Most of the lads built tables and chairs out of wood, and lockers out of cardboard boxes. The toilets were of two designs, pee tubes were sunk into the desert floor – everyone called them desert roses, because they had a funnel at the top and looked like roses growing in the desert. The main loos were of wooden construction, with three toilet seats and 45-gallon oil drums cut in half and placed under to catch the waste. A couple of the lads were detailed off to burn the waste every day; they got paid extra for being the 'Shit Burners'. The showers were made up of various things – including NBC decontamination kits, they seemed to keep everyone clean however. I had managed to convince a sergeant storeman from the US Marine Corps to give me 200 cot beds; I went to pick them up with Dave Bedford, one of the crewmen, when the Colonel of the unit came out and asked what was going on. I explained we were from a Royal Navy commando squadron, he was happy with that, but was more interested in my SA80 rifle and, as part exchange for the cots, he asked for a Naval beret, so I made Dave give his. The Colonel was over the moon with that, so all was sweet. When Dave and I got back to the FOB, I gave every man on the squadron a cot, we had quite a few left over, so I gave the rest to our sister squadron 845, who were co-located with us near KKMC.

The air war continued at pace and one day a Scud air-raid warning red came in, that's the highest threat. Just after the warning, there was a load whoosh. About 1,000m away from our site was a US based Patriot missile battery. The Scud was coming close and the Patriot missiles were fired off; seconds later there was a load bang. The Patriot had either hit its target or been blown up by its operator in mid-air. Bits of tin and shrapnel rained down all over the place; we were all suited up but waited until we got the chemical all clear before standing down from the highest NBC state, just in case the Scud had been full of chemicals.

After about three weeks the air war was approaching its conclusion, the troops, tanks, guns and attack helicopters were forming up near the Iraq border. There was a berm (soil/sand bank) all along the border and this would have to be breached before any ground attack could take place.

Flying over the desert we saw troops and encampments everywhere, all ready to break through and attack the Iraqi soldiers and tanks. Our main roles were troop movement and casevac (casualty evacuation). This we had practised quite a lot, initially with the aircraft converted to an ambulance that had six stretchers, three fitted on either side of the cabin. I had performed a test flight a couple of nights earlier, wearing AR5 and NVG (night vision goggles). The sortie lasted five hours and was hot, hard work, getting bodies in and out of the aircraft on stretchers. Eventually the sweat in the AR5 built up and was hanging around my neck seal, then – of all the times for it happen – I had a nose bleed (I was prone to nose bleeds then); the blood was streaming out of my nose and into my AR5, mixing with the sweat and around my face mask, not comfortable at all and there was no way to take the AR5 off with a helmet and NVG on. I pressed the nose excluder down (much like a nose clip for diving) and eventually managed to stem the blood flow.

When the sortie was complete, I got the AR5 off and took it to our safety equipment section, who look after our flying clothing, and explained what had happened. They cleaned the AR5 out and said afterwards what a pain in the neck it had been getting all the blood and sweat out from the nooks and crannies, but thankfully they had made it ready for my next flight. That same day, one of the pilots from 845 Squadron was cleaning his 9mm pistol in his accommodation tent. He had cleaned the pistol, rebuilt it, loaded it and then, while checking it, had a 'negligent discharge', i.e. accidentally fired a round off. The line of fire was straight into another pilot's bed and sleeping bag, which had been occupied not two minutes beforehand. Fortunately, it was not occupied when the pistol was fired. The pilot was not normally prone to negligence, this was just a genuine oversight and a hard lesson learnt.

The following day, 6 March, we were everywhere; in the desert, to the coast, down the MSR and flying Kate Adie around with her camera man. The Prime Minister was visiting and we were also flying the press around, we had to pre-position Kate in the desert for John Major's visit. The aircraft landed at the pre-recced site and I got Kate and her cameraman out through the back door; they climbed out but didn't move away from the door. I waved them away, trying to explain what would happen if they didn't move, but they weren't worried, so I cleared the pilot for take off. As we lifted, the recirculation and downwash from the blades started to blow the sand all around the aircraft. It was like a very large sand blasting machine, dust and particles flying everywhere and in the middle of all of it was Kate and her cameraman, their bodies and equipment being pebble-dashed and stripped clean by sand. I would meet Kate a few times throughout my flying career and each time I would remind her of that incident – she always took it in good spirit.

As aircrewmen, we are responsible for the GPMG in the back of the aircraft and the need to remain competent in its operation and drills. To that end we had set up a range to carry out some practice firings. The range was in the middle of the desert, about five miles from KKMC, and was a park for abandoned lorries and buses. There were five of us in the back of the aircraft and we had 400 rounds each to fire, the first crewman took aim as we flew past the range, I called for the target to be a yellow bus in the middle of all the vehicles and we ran in at about 80 knots and opened fire. The rounds started to go down towards the bus (one tracer round in every four rounds, so you can see the fall of shot); we had fired about 200 rounds when all of a sudden a couple of animals came out, goats I think, then a herdsman followed, I called a halt to the firing. He was a lucky man, the range had been cleared, but obviously this man had escaped by hiding in the bus. We moved him out of the area and started firing again, this time without incident.

When we woke up the next day, no dawn broke; the sky was black. The Iraqis forces had torched the oil fields in Kuwait and the sky was covered in a thick acrid smoke, it was like some picture from a sci-fi movie, with cloud and smoke all swirling around in circles and long columns. At 11 o'clock in the morning we still needed torches and lights to operate. Eventually it cleared slightly with a change of wind direction, but it took a long time before the fires were finally extinguished.

The day of the race came at last, the air war had done its job and the land war was about to start. Our main task was medevac for our troops. The berm was breached and the tanks and vehicles flowed through. The main conflict was taking place between the Iraqi tanks and the attack helicopters, (Apaches and the Army Lynx), the helicopters were winning and destroying everything in sight. A couple of days passed, the work was intense, with long hours and it was very hot during the day, but cold at night. There were a lot of medevac sorties, but more for the Iraqi troops than coalition forces. The front line started to move north toward the Kuwait/Iraq border.

As the advance gathered more momentum, there were more and more prisoners of war scattered around the desert, they were hot, thirsty and wanted to surrender. We ended up picking them up from all over the desert and taking the PoWs to holding camps. Eventually all the Iraqis had to be moved into Saudi, to a camp near KKMC; as we moved them it struck me that there was a smell, a smell that I had known before in 1982 when moving Argentine prisoners of war. Even though the Falklands War had been in the winter and over 8,000 miles away from Iraq, the smell was exactly the same. Some people say it's the smell of defeat or the odour of men who have either given up or finally relaxed because their war is over. It is a distinct scent that I will never forget.

The advance had gone well, with the Iraqi troops and vehicles heading north or captured. Then the advance was halted; we had moved into Iraq and the squadron set up a new advanced FOB due west of the Kuwait border. We had flown deeper into Saddam country, over the main Iraqi gun emplacements and trenches. It was like something out of the First World War in the Somme: zig zag trenches and deep pits to hide in when the bombardments came in from the Allied forces. As we advanced through the trenches, we landed and I picked up an Iraqi gas mask in its original carry bag; first I checked it for booby traps and then we made our way to our new FOB site and carried on tasking and picking up more prisoners of war.

The next sortie we were tasked to carry out was to take the press into Kuwait and along the Basra road. The coalition forces had destroyed a convoy of hundreds of Iraqi vehicles that had been trying to escape north from the city, back to their homeland. I had the press on board, a cameraman and a couple of reporters, one from the BBC and one from ITV. As we flew towards Kuwait City the smoke from the remains of the still-burning vehicles was rising into the late afternoon sky. I asked Nige North, who was flying, to come low down over the Basra road, the devastation was immense. Hundreds of wrecked tanks, armoured personnel carriers (APC), buses, cars and trucks. There were bodies scattered everywhere, some burnt and some with limbs missing. I got the cameraman to the door, but even though he was strapped in by a harness, he would not come all the way to the door, so I did the filming for him. To this day I am not sure if it was the scene of the devastation or the door opening that put the cameraman off, only he knows. I also took loads of shots on my camera for our records. I sent these back to RNAS Yeovilton, but I never saw them again.

Later that day, Nige, Sergeant Bob Holmwood, Lieutenant Steve 'Thumper' Powell and I drove into Kuwait City via the Basra road. A lot of the bodies had been removed but there were still many lying on the ground. We stopped and got out for a walk around; Nige wandered off to the edge of the carriageway and I followed as he went towards a partially destroyed

APC. As he approached it I spotted a wire strung across the walkway between the APC and a car, I shouted for Nige to stop and fortunately he did. We looked more closely at the wire and found that attached to one end of it was a grenade. This was a very quickly constructed booby trap and Nige had nearly walked straight into it. We marked the booby trap and told the RMP troops who were guarding the area about it. Then we drove into the Kuwait City and down to two 614ft towers known as 'the Onion towers' by the Gulf coast, where I picked up a couple of empty 30mm shell cases from a gun emplacement to take home after the war, taking care again that they were not booby trapped.

The next day, the announcement was made that we had stopped fighting and would not advance any further. It was then that we started taking the squadron engineers around the operating area to show them some of the sights. We flew down the Basra road, but most of the vehicles had been pushed off the road, then we flew around Kuwait City, down the coast and into the oil fields, showing the burning oil wells. Finally, we went inland to where several tanks had been destroyed and were making our way at low level back to the FOB, flying at about 100ft so the lads could see the desert surface, when all of a sudden there was a huge explosion directly under our aircraft. It threw the aircraft up and to the left – we had set off a tank mine; immediately we checked the aircraft for damage, I could not see any and Nige said all the systems and engines were OK. Lucky escape again, I thought. We flew on for about another mile and landed on a nearby road to carry out a physical check of the underside of the helicopter. Everything was OK, so we made our way back to the FOB for the engineers to do some in-depth checks of the aircraft.

During the Gulf War all aircrews had been given ten gold sovereigns each and a promissory note worth £15,000. These were to be used if you ended up either shot down or captured by the Bedouins. The idea was to give the coins to your captors and persuade them to return you to the coalition forces, where they could also get cash for the promissory note.

Now hostilities had ceased, all the gold sovereigns and promissory notes had to be collected up and flown down to Riyadh, the capital. The main British HQ was there and we were tasked to fly the box of coins and notes, worth well over £4 million, back to Riyadh and stay overnight in a 5-star hotel – luxury! I was looking forward to that. We flew down to Riyadh, parked the aircraft up at the airport and went to the HQ to deliver our package. My medic and I carried the box into the main operations' room, we had been in the desert for about ten weeks and I think we may have smelled a little awful, because when we walked in to their nice clean and tidy ops room, the ops teams looked at us as though we had come down from the moon. We had our weapons on still, the doc had his 9mm Browning pistol and I had both a 9mm and an SA80 Rifle. Perhaps they were a little concerned, as Riyadh was the closest they had all been to the front line during the whole of the war. We delivered the box and then set off for the hotel. Nige North, Thumper Powel, the doc and. I hadn't slept in a proper bed for ages and when I got to my room I found, in the middle of a vast bedroom, a round super-king-size bed; it was huge. The hotel was fantastic. Being in Saudi it was dry and no alcohol was available; not a problem, but it would have been nice to have had a beer in such an amazing place. I had a proper shower, which was great, and then got into bed. Could I sleep though? It was too comfortable, I had been sleeping on a clicky bed and in a sleeping bag for so long, I just could not get to sleep. Eventually, I took all the bedding off the bed, slept on the carpet and covered myself with the duvet from the bed. It was the only way I could get a good night's kip!

When we arrived back at the squadron FOB site, we were told that the following week we would embark our aircraft into RFA *Argus* for the return journey back to the UK. The hospital ship *Argus* was alongside at Al Jubail at the time and would sail back to the UK two weeks later with all the aircraft, but we would fly back from Saudi to Brize Norton in a British Airways Boeing 747. We left Iraq on 18 March; another war survived and more stories (Dits) to tell.

We got quite a good reception when we finally arrived home, nothing like coming back from the Falklands but still nice. Most importantly I was back with Cath, who was happy that I had returned safe and sound again. Then it was time for Easter leave and back to work. The first sortie after leave was to go to RFA *Argus,* which had now returned from the Gulf, and pick up our aircraft then fly them back to Yeovilton. It was a bit sad really, 848 had been such a good squadron and the men on there were great, a real bunch of 'Kelly's Hero's', a bunch of misfits and misplaced characters from the Fleet Air Arm commando units and squadrons, and now after such a short time we were going to disband. The squadron had been put together at short notice and would de-commission in short time also. The lads from 848 would return to their units or squadrons, the end of another era for 848 Squadron. Nige North, Tim Lort, J.F.R. Evans and I would leave the squadron to re-form the Clockwork cell and instruct Arctic operations again up in Norway at Bardufoss.

Chapter 11

It was now June 1992 and UK training continued at pace, after a lull while we had been away in the Gulf. Most of the aircraft had been deployed, but a small team was left behind to continue training and cover for our Special Forces UK commitments and tasks.

The Clockwork cell personnel, when not out in Norway, were all employed as instructors on 707 Squadron, which was the training unit. This enabled us to keep our hand in and remain current in commando operations. My role in the Clockwork cell ended at the end of October 1992, when I was drafted to the Naval Flying Standard Flight at Yeovilton. This was one of the pinnacles of an aircrewman's career path and it was an honour to be appointed as the Commando Standards Aircrewman based at Yeovilton.

I look back now and I had followed in a certain aircrewman's footsteps. I had looked up to Alf Tupper and now I had done almost all the same jobs as he had done before me. He had been there and got all the ticks in all of the boxes, plus he was highly respected by everyone in the Naval helicopter world. The final accolade came from a Petty Office Aircrewman when he was being 'trapped'; he said I was his Alf Tupper, and that said it all for me, to be compared to Alf, that was truly an honour.

I joined Standards (trappers) at the beginning of November 1992, with 4,700 flying hours, in many different types of helicopter. I was qualified as a commando, ASW and SAR crewman, plus I had done four years test flying and was a qualified NVG, MCT, helicopter abseil and fast roping instructor.

I hoped I had all the street cred to do the job as a trapper.

Even though I had left the Clockwork cell and joined Standards, I was still employed in Norway as an Arctic flying instructor during my 'non-trapping' weeks; the workload in Bardufoss was quite heavy due to lots of aircrew needing to requalify after our efforts in the Gulf the previous winter. The best thing about this for me was that I could get some skiing in at night when we weren't flying or out in the field.

Trappers were always seen as the bad boys of the aviation world, always trying to catch people out (i.e. trap them into doing something wrong). During his term as trapper though, Alf Tupper had started to put that myth to bed. Brian Johnson had done the same and, hopefully, I continued that theme as I attempted to teach as well as examine, which was a more constructive way of trapping and letting aircrewmen learn from my own experience.

I settled into the job and with my pilots, Lieutenant Ian 'Laps' Chapman and then Lieutenant Jerry Spence, we made quite a good team. The remainder of the year was taken up with visiting different squadrons in the Fleet Air Arm bases at, Culdrose, Portland, Yeovilton and Prestwick.

The flying was very varied and the level of expertise among the crewmen and observers I had to test was normally very high. Some took me a bit for granted though. My opposite number down at RNAS Culdrose was WOACMN Terry King, he was the ASW trapper but still helped me out doing the commando squadron traps. I was quite experienced as an ASW operator, but some of the new crewmen on the squadrons didn't realise that, they thought I was only commando qualified. Subsequently they would try to pull the wool over my eyes. They soon realised that was not the way ahead and the word quickly spread that I was fully qualified in all aspects of crewman aviation.

1992 was a pretty good year and I was at home quite a lot. Kieran was now 16 years old, and Simon was 14; both were doing well at Wellington school. By this stage, Cath was working as a supervisor at Pioneer, the Co-Op superstore. We were still living in married quarters in Yeovil, but hoped to sell our house in Cornwall before too long and buy again in Somerset.

Eventually we did sell our house in Godolphin Cross, for a very small profit, and started looking for a house near Yeovilton. A house came up, in the village of Yeovilton, at the back of the Air Station. It was nice, but at the time I thought it was a little too close to the airfield. Cath loved it and convinced me that we should buy so three days later we put in a reasonable bid and the offer was accepted. We moved into the house in time for the Christmas of 1992 and after twenty-eight years we are still here, so it must have been the right place to buy.

There was not a lot going on in the trapping world during January 1993, so I helped out with some fighter evasion and flying instruction on 707 Squadron. February was also pretty quiet, then I got a visit from John Spencer, the Chief Aircrewman of 845 Squadron. 845 were on an operational deployment with the United Nations (UN) in Bosnia.

CHAPTER 11

He said that one of his parents was very ill and near death, and if I was not too busy could I go out to Bosnia in his place for a month detachment. I looked at the calendar and asked Cath if she minded too much, she said not. My programme at Standards Flight was not busy, so I agreed to stand in for him. I went to Brize Norton in mid-February and flew out on an RAF VC10 to Split airfield in Croatia, to join the 845 Detachment based in Divulje Barracks, about two miles from the airport on the Adriatic coast. The flying there was great, the UN had us doing many varied tasks. However the frustrating thing was that it was a passive role. The war was on going all around us, but we could not really do anything. Our hands were tied.

On one sortie we had to go to Kiseljak, the main UN headquarters to the North West of Sarajevo. We had taken two aircraft, landed and then went into the main building which overlooked the main road running through Kiseljak town. We were on the top floor of the five-storey building looking down on the town centre. From the south along the main road came a ZSU 57/2 (a 57mm, twin-barrelled, self-propelled anti-aircraft gun). It trundled along the road, came halfway into the town and stopped; it lowered its barrels, turned the guns towards a house (we were told a family of Bosnian Muslims were in there) and fired a sustained burst of 57mm shells straight into the house, totally destroying the building and killing all inside. Not one of us could do a thing about it, and neither could the UN troops on the ground. What an awful feeling, of being total ineffectual and unable to help in any way.

On 16 March, we had a royal visitor, Prince Charles. He came to the squadron and we were to fly him into Bosnia, up to Sarajevo and then down to the coast via the Mostar bridge, which had been destroyed, and finally back to Divulje Barracks. As we flew, I reminded him about his/our time on 845 in the early 1970s. It was nice to have some common ground that we could reminisce about.

I was due to fly home on 26 March, having been out in the former Yugoslavia for a month. On the 25th, however, an immediate task came in. The task was to fly into Srebrenica and evacuate injured refugees and children from the Muslim enclave. A detachment of three aircraft flew up to Kiseljak, we left one aircraft there and then with three crews flew up to Tuzla, near the Serbian border. The briefing took place with the French Army Pumas which were also involved. We would fly into Srebrenica via Zvornik in Serbia, in order to be searched by the Serbians before they would allow us to go into the Srebrenica enclave. The search at Zvornik was tense but uneventful.

We lifted from Zvornik, behind the French Pumas, who would go in first. The French had gone ahead to insert our landing site team, led by my old mate Tim Kelly from 846 in the Falklands, he was now a Lieutenant working as the lead on the Mobile Air Operations Team. He would control the LZ when we landed and withdrew the children and refugees.

The Serbians had given us assurance that they would not shell the enclave while we were carrying out the rescue. All was good as we approached the LZ, so we landed and got as many refugees as we could into the back of the aircraft. We were just about to lift when that sound started, a sound I had heard many times before. Over the noise of the rotors came THUMP, THUMP, BOOM, BOOM. The Bosnian Serbs had started shelling us, they had gone back on their word. We lifted and got out as quickly as we could, making our way back to Tuzla where they were expecting us. As we landed, vehicles came out to meet us, ambulances, lorries and APCs to help all the injured, sick and elderly refugees. I had a small baby in my arms and gave her over to one of the medics. It was then that I saw Kate Adie and I thought this must be real if she is here, it's like old times all over again.

After shutting the aircraft down we went for a debrief with General Morillon the UN military commander of Bosnia. It was then that we heard that the shelling in Srebrenica had continued and several of the UN troops had been hit and needed evacuating ASAP. The French declined to go back in, but our boss, Lieutenant Commander George Wallace, said we would go. So, after a refuel, we set out again, via Zvornik and into Srebrenica. This time, though, Tim radioed to us that the original LZ was still under fire and we would have to winch the casualties from the centre of town, by the AT&T building near the main square.

We, that was George Wallace, Flight Lieutenant Brian Smith an RAF exchange pilot, my medic and I would go in and do the rescue, while Lieutenant Kev Smith and Sergeant Steve Humphries would provide top cover overhead Srebrenica. As we approached the site I could see the devastation of the town. There were people everywhere; this was a town of 6,000 inhabitants and there was at least 60,000 down there now and they all wanted to get on this helicopter.

We settled into a hover and I made a quick assessment of the area. There were telephone and power cables everywhere, but I spotted one area that we could winch from. We called Tim Kelly on the radio and informed him where to go to enable us to start winching the injured up. I lowered the first stretcher and recovered a casualty, a Canadian soldier with severe shrapnel injuries to the side of his head; the second casualty was not much better.

Then the thumps of the rounds started to get closer again. I had five more guys to bring up, but they were walking wounded. The last would be Tim. He was on the ground holding a 3-year-old girl who was bleeding badly and not in a good way. I lowered the winch to recover them both, but as the strop got to Tim he handed the girl back to her mother. She had died in his arms. I felt for him, as at the time he had a 3-year-old daughter of his own. He put the strop under his arms and I raised him as the thumps got steadily, closer and louder. Tim looked devastated as I pulled him into the aircraft and we departed that town for the last time, leaving all those people hoping we would come back for them; unfortunately, that wasn't going to happen.

The task was completed, Brian had flown the aircraft superbly and we had rescued our guys from an area where the most horrific events would take place later on in the war. As we landed at Tuzla, again the ambulances were there and so was Kate Adie. She interviewed Tim, but he could hardly speak; he was really upset as you can imagine. We had just shut the rotors down when I heard that familiar sound. The buggers were now starting to shell us at Tuzla airfield. Everyone rushed to take shelter in the waiting armoured vehicles for safety. The aircraft were hit with shrapnel but no real damage was done. Then to top it all off it started to snow; not just light snow either, really heavy stuff, so thick that we were going nowhere. I am supposed to be going home tomorrow, I thought. That's not going to happen, is it? Cath will be really happy, late back again. That's never happened before has it? Or maybe it has. I phoned her about an hour later, she had been worried when she found out I was on the Srebrenica rescue, which had been all over the world news.

The snow lasted till 28 March, we were stuck in Tuzla barracks and each day at 5am and 5pm we were shelled from the hills on the border of Serbia. Finally we managed to grovel out at low level and fly back to Divulje Barracks in Croatia. The following day I flew home to Yeovilton; Cath was happy that I had eventually got home and was due some leave at last.

I continued in my job as the trapper and I must admit, even though I was going around examining crewmen in their specific roles, I learnt a lot from them too over the months of testing. In July I went back out to Bosnia again for the month; the weather was fantastic and the flying good, control had been handed over from the UN to IFOR (NATO Implementation Forces). Simon Thornewill (my ex-boss) visited while I was there, he was now a Captain and a senior staff officer. The senior pilot of 845 was Dave Lord so, including me, that was three of the crew from our incident in the Falklands when we were shot at by the A4s (shame Alf Tupper could not be there).

Dave Lord and I flew Simon around the Bosnian war zone, it was nice to be back together and reminisce about past times.

Divulje Barracks was right on the coast of the Adriatic, about fifteen miles west of Split. The water was lovely there and 845 had a benefactor in Sir Donald Gosling, the owner of NCP car parks. Sir Donald was an ex-matelot, he knew where we were and amazingly he donated £25,000 to the squadron, to be spent on adventurous training equipment. The cash went into buying a RIB (rigid inflatable boat) and water skis, three sailing dinghies and some wind surf boards. These were well used. I had skied on snow before, but never on water. I managed to get up on the second attempt. The water was perfect for skiing in the morning and then when the wind got up in the afternoon perfect for sailing and windsurfing. So, if you weren't flying or working, the place to be was out on the water. Thanks to Sir Donald Gosling.

I managed one more tour in Bosnia during my time on NFSF at Yeovilton, I enjoyed getting back to the front line, but knew that my time on Standards would soon come to an end. Then, towards the end of 1993, the promotion letter to Warrant Officer came out. There were to be two CPOACMN promoted: one was an ASW Chief called John Cooper and I was the other. Finally, I had achieved most of what I could aspire to, a job as the Standards crewman and soon be promoted to Warrant Officer. The rest of the year flew by, working at Culdrose, Yeovilton and Portland, with an extra plus that by the end of 1993 I had also achieved 5,000 flying hours, a small feat in itself.

Chapter 12

The start of 1994 came about and when I went back to work after leave at NFSF I joined as a Warrant Officer which was a great feeling, to get to the pinnacle of the Aircrewman's branch. Funny how people treat you slightly differently when you are a Warrant Officer! The first half of the year was taken up with trapping and training students on 707 Squadron. Just before leave though I had to go and see the appointer, who drafts Warrant Officers. He suggested I should move to an aircraft carrier and do an operations job. I suggested he change his mind, as I would not do that and would resign my Warrant if he sent me. He changed his mind and offered me the post of Senior Crewman on 819 Squadron at HMS *Gannet* near Prestwick in Scotland. This was an ASW unit, but within the unit was based an SAR flight that covered the West Coast of Scotland. I accepted and joined there after a short course to convert me to the newish Mk6 Sea King ASW Aircraft, which was now based at 819 Squadron. So, my time on standards flight came to an end; I think I achieved a lot during my period there, but it was nice to move on and get back to the front line – albeit an ASW/SAR front-line unit.

After summer leave I completed my conversion at RNAS Culdrose and then travelled up to Scotland to join my new squadron. Cath had decided she would not move with me, so I would have to commute every other weekend. I settled in to my cabin in the Warrant Officers' and Senior Rates' accommodation, which was fine. The job was slightly different to what I had been used to and, as the Warrant Officer on the squadron, I was the Divisional Officer (DO) and reporting officer for all of my junior rating aircrewman, I also had the roles of the passive Sonar Training Officer, the Military Training Officer (from my commando crewman role), the Sports Officer and the DO to the Petty Officer PTI. In addition to these roles, because of my experience and the fact that I was already SAR Qualified and had just left standards, I was employed in teaching the SAR courses to the crewmen and observers on the SAR Flight, plus I ended up doing watches on the flight also. So quite a heavy workload. But the squadron and personnel were great, the flying around the Scottish mountains was really good. The SAR call outs happened all the time and we were one of the busiest rescue flights around the country, due to our patch being coastal and mountainous, which meant I had to shuffle my time between SAR and ASW. I enjoyed them both, but commando flying was still my thing!

It was now approaching autumn and the rugby season was starting. I had given up playing the previous year because injuries and age were taking their toll. My last game had been a fathers' and sons' match, where Kieran, Simon and I had scored a try each. The next thing I knew, I was being asked to play rugby for Prestwick because they were short of experience in the back row. Begrudgingly I said yes. I played No.8 and scored two tries; the next week I was named as captain. My rugby career started again and I was really enjoying it. The rest of the year was filled with more SAR training, SAR watches and rugby – I even started playing golf and my game was improving. One day we had an SAR Scramble to Barassie Golf course, where a member was suffering a cardiac arrest. We arrived, stabilised him and took him to Glasgow Royal Infirmary, where he made a full recovery. By way of thank you for saving him, the club gave us a free 4-ball every Wednesday afternoon. We made use of it because even in 1995 it was £40 per round and something we didn't want to lose.

I had done the RAF winter survival course a few years beforehand and while I was on 819 I was offered the chance to do another course on survival, but this time it would be in Norway. Not run by the Brits, but by the Norwegians, at a small resort near Fagernes. This course lasted two weeks and was set up by the Ace Mobile Force, which included most of the NATO forces. On the course were French, Americans, Norwegians, Germans, Brits and many more nationalities. The Brits included two Royal Marine pilots (Steve Piddle and Dee Irvine) who I knew quite well; a Lynx pilot (Mike Clarke) and me. The other three had come from Yeovilton and me from Prestwick. The course involved flying to Oslo, where we had the weekend in a hotel, then topped up with booze from the Embassy for the two weeks ahead (all the nations did that), followed by a bus trip to the resort. This was not going to be a strenuous survival exercise.

As part of the kit list we had to take our Mess Undress, that meant either a mess dinner or cocktail party. The first night was the cocktail party, so all the nations provided some booze and got to know each other. Then each night after, apart from two evenings, each nation put on a party (really difficult survival course…). The two nights when there was no party were spent out in the field, with one night in a snow hole. That was pretty simple; Steve, Dee and I had all been to Norway many times and completed Arctic Warfare Training, so Mike had quite an easy ride. The second night was spent in an individual shelter; we had been given a parachute each, with which we had to erect a shelter and make a sleeping bag. The helicopter operators found this quite easy, but the fixed-wing pilots struggled a bit. An Italian pilot was chopping wood with a machete to build a fire; it was cold and he misjudged his swing, missing the branch and chopping into his leg. We administered first aid, but the cut was pretty bad, so we had to take him to the staff and he was whisked off to hospital. That was the end of the course for him. The last evening consisted of a mess dinner. I can honestly say this was the most relaxed and enjoyable survival course I had ever been on. On returning back to 819, I sang the praises of the course and told the other guys that they should apply for it next year.

The commuting up and down the UK was taking its toll with everyone. Most of the lads who lived in England commuted every weekend, some, like me, every other weekend. Most had been involved in some sort of accident during their time at Prestwick, either self-induced or someone else's bad driving and it was no different for me. I was driving up the M6 just north of Charnock Richard services in Lancashire one Sunday evening, it was just after dusk and I was returning to HMS *Gannet*. The road was fairly clear, there had been a shower of rain but nothing too heavy, and it was cold. I was in the middle lane when I saw smoke pluming from the rear axle of an articulated lorry on the inside lane, and just as a precaution I started to move out into the fast lane. I was about 200 metres from the lorry when all of a sudden, a large black shape was hurtling towards me. I ducked down into the car as the thing hit me. I was still travelling at 70mph, so the impact was tremendous; it caved the roof of the car in and every piece of glass – the sun roof and all the windows – smashed into a million pieces. The noise was horrific. At first I thought I wouldn't survive the impact, but I looked up at an angle and could just see out of the front where the windscreen had been. I started to brake and came to a halt on the hard shoulder.

I looked around at total devastation. The passenger side of the roof was crushed down to the passenger seat and I could just sit up by leaning to the right. The driver of the lorry rushed up to me and asked if I was OK. As I got out of the car I cut my finger on some broken glass, and that was my only injury (another life gone). The driver told me I had been hit by the double wheel of his artic, which had seized, fractured off the lorry and bounced down the road on to my car. I had survived another major accident. The really lucky thing was that I had been due to take a passenger up that evening, but he had cried off because he was ill. If he had been with me he would have died for sure; a lucky escape for both of us.

Cath came up for a week during the summer and loved it up in Scotland. I think she would have enjoyed it permanently but the thought of moving up was too much, after only a few years in our house in Somerset. It was just as well she chose not to move in the end, because there was a development in the South of England. RNAS Portland was going to close and 772 Squadron, which was based there, would fold and be amalgamated with 707 Squadron at Yeovilton to form – you guessed it – 848 Squadron, which would become a much larger unit, training the commando aircrew of the future and also taking on the MCT (Maritime Counter Terrorism) role. Because of the enlargement of the squadron, the Commanding Officer, one Dave Lord, requested that a Warrant Officer should be in charge of the crewmen and I was going to be that man. This would be the third time I had served on 848 in three different roles, as an electrician, as the CPOACMN and now as the Warrant Officer. 819 would not release me right away, so I would have to wait until the new year before I could move and join 848 again.

Kieran was now at university in Manchester and Simon was doing his A-levels at Wellington School, so Cath was on her own in the house in Somerset. Her job as a supervisor at the Co-Op was getting her down a bit, so I suggested she apply for a civil service role at Yeovilton. She started work in the Resettlement Office, offering advice to leavers from the Royal Navy on future civilian careers. She was much happier there and enjoyed the work immensely.

I left 819 in the December of 1995; it was a sad day because I had really enjoyed my eighteen months in Scotland, but going back to Yeovilton and being able to return home to Cath most nights meant everything.

Chapter 13

January 1996 was the start of a new era for me. 848 Squadron in Yeovilton was now the biggest Mk4 Sea King Squadron on the base, and my new role and responsibilities were the most demanding of my flying career. As Warrant Officer for the squadron, I was in charge of the training for the Commando Aircrewman Operation Flying Training Course, I was also a Divisional Officer for eighteen sailors who were aircrewmen, survival equipment ratings, aircraft handlers (chock heads), chefs and stewards. This was not an easy bunch of men to look after and write up every six months.

I was also the lead crewman for the MCT role, which the squadron had inherited from 772 Squadron at Portland. I had been involved in this job previously, in 1970 when it had been set up, and more recently I had flown on many sorties in my trapper role.

I was well acquainted with the staff crewmen and pilots, and obviously knew the Commanding Officer Dave Lord very well. The senior pilot was a man called Rick Fox, a gentleman and placed in my highest estimation. It was good to be back in the commando role; the job seems more involved and is where I am most at home. I also enjoyed the routine; I would spend one week of every month away, either in the training environment or on an MCT task. The other weeks would be spent day- and night-flying, writing reports and doing divisional work, which took up more of my time than it should have. The lads in my division were … how can I put it? They liked to live life to the full – i.e. they got into trouble quite a lot. On four occasions I had to attend court with them. I represented the men as their 'accused friend' and Divisional Officer; I tried to speak up for them and explain that they regretted what they had done and would be good boys in the future. It worked sometimes, but not all the time!

Some evenings I got home late due to the heavy workload, but this was still better than commuting from Scotland and the late work wasn't every night. After I had been on the squadron for about five months things were settled, the courses were ticking through and the MCT task was steady. Dave Lord announced that he was moving on to pastures new and I wondered who was going to take over from him. About a week later I bumped into Steve Daniels, who had been on 846 with me in the early 1980s and also at RWTS Boscombe Down. He let slip to me that he was going to be my next boss, but to keep it quiet. I was over the moon at the news. Dave had been a good boss, but having Steve Daniels as my CO and Rick Fox as the SP, would be exceptional – a leadership team made in heaven.

The squadron had a new lease of life when Steve took over; we moved into a new squadron building, with modern rooms and briefing facilities. The joint crew room in the old building though had given us the ability to communicate on a social level with the pilots and even discuss our students performances away from the formal briefing and de-briefing regime, whereas the down side to the new building was that the crewmen had a separate crew room facilities from the pilots and that social interaction that existed previously had disappeared. But new block, new system.

The courses were now rolling through; ten weeks for each course then a fresh group of students started again. Work was busy and another extra role for me was as head of the Commando Aircrewman Branch drafting and future development. This involved consideration of the role and the way ahead for the commando lads at Yeovilton. Bill Baily, a Warrant Officer aircrewman working for the Flag Officer Naval Aviation (FONA), was doing the same for the ASW Crewmen throughout the Fleet Air Arm. His agenda was a little different to mine though. He wanted to make all Royal Navy aircrewmen ASW and all commando aircrewmen Royal Marines. I was totally against this happening. A certain commander from Royal Naval Manning had endorsed Bill's idea and was now starting to implement the plan. It was all wrong as far as I was concerned and not good for the Naval commando aircrewmen. I argued the case for RN aircrewmen to stay in the commando role, but eventually I hit a brick wall; Bill and the Naval Manning Commander would not consider my objections. They would not change their tack at all.

In the good old tradition of the Royal Navy, I wrote a service paper to put my point of view to FONA. The paper laid down all the salient points; the pros and cons of Bill Baily's intentions and manning requirements, the fact that the Royal Marines could never commit to sufficient manpower, and the impact on Naval aircrewmen in the commando role.

I put the paper into Steve Daniels who corrected some points for me, then it went to Commodore Scott Ledbetter, Yeovilton's Station Commanding Officer.

CHAPTER 13

To my amazement, the next day Commodore Ledbetter phoned me and asked me to go and see him. I again put my case to him and he agreed with all the points I had raised and agreed to forward my paper to FONA. Again, I was amazed to get a phone call from FONA Admiral Sir Desmond Cassidi, who asked me to go and see him. I presented my case to him in the same way I had done with Scott Ledbetter and he told me to leave it with him. The following day he informed me that the change suggested by Naval Manning and Bill had been put to bed and would not happen. Great! I had got my way for the better of the Commando Aircrewman Branch. But at what cost?

Steve Daniels called me in a couple of days later and said that the Commander Naval Manning had a long knife out for me because I had stopped his plan coming to fruition. This could affect my career in the following two years – or maybe even help me. Only time would tell.

Work was intense over the next few months, but the squadron grew in esteem with its management of the training regime and fulfilment of the MCT role. The squadron saw a steady stream of RN and RM aircrewmen and pilots filtering through on the courses; some did well but others did not, and that was when my job took on a less enjoyable turn. Having to tell a hopeful student, the week before they were due to graduate following eighteen months of demanding training, that they had failed was not a pleasurable task. Sometimes they were just relieved it was all over, while others were gutted and didn't take failure well at all, which is hardly surprising.

Our oldest son Kieran had been studying Engineering at university in Manchester, which was probably the wrong course for him. He did OK in the first year, but then contracted glandular fever, which killed his chances of studying. During his time in Manchester he also completed the aptitude tests to join the RN as a pilot and had done quite well, but then came the medical. It was discovered that he was colour blind, which put paid to him becoming a pilot in the Royal Navy; I was gutted for him. He continued to study, but was way behind on the course studies as a consequence of the glandular fever.

While at university, he had joined the Officer Training Corps (OTC) and was enjoying his time with that unit. When it came to decision time about his future, Kieran chose to give up his degree course and join the Army. He passed the Army Officers board and arrived at Sandhurst, the Army Officers training college, the day after his 21st birthday. To this day I believe he has not regretted making that choice.

Kieran has now progressed to Lieutenant Colonel and is the Commanding Officer of a Royal Artillery Regiment. When he did his Senior Staff Course he also gained a master's degree, so in the end he achieved his academic qualification.

About the same time Kieran was joining the Army, Simon was starting a degree course in Sports Science; he was going to join the Royal Navy as a Principal War Officer, but eventually decided it was not for him and went down the route of teaching, ending up as the director of sport at a private prep school in Somerset. Cath and I are extremely proud of both our sons' achievements.

Back at the squadron, the commando flying course always ends with a Military Training Exercise (MILEX), which is also their final flying test. If they pass that week then they normally progress to the front line. On one occasion the course was carrying out its MILEX on Salisbury Plain, it involved troop moves, load lifting, fighter evasion, ground military training and lots of planning for combat, all carried out during the day and night. I was flying one night with Lieutenant Griffin and an Italian exchange student called Franco; we were doing a night sortie and lifting out of a confined area in a wood. Griff was flying and Franco was the second pilot, but in the right-hand seat. We were flying on night-vision goggles and as we lifted from between the trees, Franco decided to check the outside air temperature gauge, which was at the top of the centre window screen near the engine throttles. Franco took out his torch and as he shone it on the temperature gauge he knocked the right engine throttle back to ground idle. I was standing behind the pilots and could see what Franco had done. Griff called engine failure. I told him what had happened and that I was advancing the number two throttle; as I did this we regained flight and rotor speed. We continued to lift clear of the trees, did a circuit round to the LZ and then landed.

The debrief was an interesting one, as Franco tried to explain what he had done. Griff thanked me and then took Franco out for a chat. I can only imagine how that went. Franco passed in the end and went to 845 Squadron and eventually became a flight commander.

The next eighteen months carried on as usual, training, MCT, court cases, Divisional Officers work, write ups and trying to keep as fit as possible. I then got a call from the appointer – the man who runs my career and resides in the Naval Command Headquarters, in Portsmouth; luckily it was not the Naval Manning section! I had to see him to discuss my next and future appointments. He suggested that I had done all the flying jobs I could do as a Warrant Officer and would be given a staff job next. I was not happy about this, as I like to be at the sharp end: flying in aircraft, rather than flying a desk. He then offered me a job as the Operations Officer 2 on 845, this was normally an officer's job. I would go there as Ops 2 and Senior Aircrewman, but only for a year.

Around that time there had been a lot of talk about where aircrewmen could be employed, and as a commando crewman we were really limited to Yeovilton or a ground-based job. I had discussed this fact with Flight Lieutenant John Heald, who was our RAF exchange officer on 848. He was going up to RAF Innsworth the following week for a meeting when he mentioned my case to the RAF Loadmaster Appointer; the following day the appointer phoned me. He asked me if I was happy with my Naval career path and had I ever thought of going across to the RAF. I said I was happy with the Navy, but not with my future employment. Apparently he had spoken with John Heald and suggested that I think about transferring to the RAF because they were short of crewmen/loadmasters. He explained I could go over as a Master Aircrew (Warrant Officer 1), either go to SAR or to Support helicopters (but only Chinook) and stay flying until I was 55 years old, which would give me an extra 5 years' work beyond that which the RN had offered me. It certainly was something to think about!

He asked about my experience so I told him I had 6,000 hours, I was an A2 Qualified Aircrew Instructor, an NVG, MCT, Abseil and Fast-roping Instructor, plus I had 400 flying hours in Chinooks. At that he asked if I wanted to join tomorrow! That wasn't an option; if I did transfer to the RAF it would take a while to get permission from the RN and first of all, I would have to consult Cath about my future career, where I would be based and for how long. I said I would get back to him. Cath was OK with the idea of me moving over to the RAF, but did not want to move if I went to RAF Odiham, where the Chinooks were based; for the price of our four-bedroom detached house, we would be lucky to get a three-bedroom semi in the Odiham area.

So I considered my prospects. In March of 1998 I would be going to 845, but that was a desk job, with a little flying. It was then that I opted for the RAF transfer. I made sure that I had a confirmed appointment in the Royal Air Force and then put the paperwork in to the Royal Navy.

Unbelievably I could not transfer, due to the fact that the RN is the Senior Service and you cannot transfer to a junior service. All I could do was to apply for what is called a Premature Release to join another Service (Voluntary Transfer in any other words). I then forwarded the paperwork to my CO, Steve Daniels; he was astonished, but realised why I was doing it. He signed the request, which then went to the Station Commander, Commodore Scott Ledbetter.

We had a coffee together and I explained to the station commander why I was making the move; that I would have a longer career and continue flying. I assured him the Royal Navy had done nothing wrong, and if they had offered me the same option as the RAF, I would have stayed. He agreed and wished me luck in my future employment. The next stage was to get the paperwork through Naval Manning at Portsmouth – my only worry was that the Commander Naval Manning had not changed. He could take his revenge on me or not, it was his call. The paperwork went in and, to my astonishment, it was approved. I could go for early release, but not for another six months, as I was about to go to the front line on 845. Commander Naval Manning had the choice to keep me in or get rid of me and he chose the latter, that was his way of getting me out of his hair.

In March I moved to 845 Squadron again. A long-time friend of mine, Mike Abbey, was the CO; we had been on standards together a few years earlier. I shared an office with Ops 1, Lieutenant Commander Jonny Pentreath. The squadron was still committed to NATO in Bosnia, and in May I went out for another tour of the former Yugoslavia. We were tasked in the casevac/rescue role from the military hospital in Sipovo, just south of Banja Luka in the northwest of Bosnia. The flying was good and we would work three days in Sipovo and three days at Divulje Barracks in Croatia, back-up tasking or taking time off. Franco had been on 845 a while now and I got to fly with him again, with no issues this time. There was a lot of physical training and runs ashore when we got the chance – it was summer and nice and hot. It was great to be back on the front line after my time on 848 Squadron in the UK. The weather and water skiing were still good. I took advantage of the opportunity to top up my CD collection from the stalls outside the Metal Factory in Banja Luka, the main HQ for British forces in Bosnia.

I returned from Bosnia to Yeovilton in June. This was followed by a trappers visit, I passed my QAI Check, then International Air day at Yeovilton, after which came summer leave.

A new ship had been commissioned by the MOD, a commando carrier called HMS *Ocean*. Not the best ship in the world; it was slow and the accommodation was not great, but it did give us another helicopter platform for the commando squadrons to work from. 845 were going to be the first squadron to operate from this deck with 3 Commando Brigade Air Squadron from the Royal Marines, who flew Scouts and Gazelles. We embarked on HMS *Ocean* for a series of sea trials; this would take us over to the Caribbean for hot weather trials. The programme would then take us to Miami and Mayport in Florida.

We sailed across the pond at an astonishingly slow 10 knots, then into Tortola in the British Virgin Islands, somewhere I had visited in 1981. We had just about enough time ashore for a couple of rum punches, then back on board ready to sail away. We were told there had been a major tornado in Honduras and Nicaragua and were heading there to help out.

On arrival, we could see that it was a major disaster; the rivers had flooded and wiped out the towns on either side of the waterway for 100 miles along the course of the river. We ended up flying 100 miles inland and taking troops and supplies into the jungle to help out, we did this for nearly two weeks. I was the Squadron Air Operations Officer as well as flying, so it was quite tiring. Working as the air ops officer and flying long hours probably don't go together, but I enjoy helping people out in those desperate situations and that's what helicopters are best at.

At the end of the two weeks we had all done a considerable amount of good work and a great deal of flying. We departed for a break in Miami, where we got in lots of golf and a couple of runs ashore. It was then that the SP told me I was going back home on the ship. I told him that I was due to leave the Navy on 31 January the following year, and as it was now the beginning of December, and I had leave to take, there was no way I was sailing back. I insisted on flying back early by civilian aircraft and flew back to the UK mid-December. I completed my leaving routine, and that was the end of my Naval career. (Or was it…?)

I did learn a lesson in humility though. As I was leaving the Royal Navy I went to the leaving desk, and a Leading Wren wanted to take my ID card off me and cut it up. That was it, she told me. I had now left the Royal Navy. After thirty years serving in Her Majesty's Royal Navy, a Leading Hand cuts up your ID card and that's it. Nobody is indispensable. I kept my ID Card intact though, as I would need it when I joined the RAF.

I eventually went off on Christmas/termination leave and had a good Christmas at home with the family. I finally had my last day in the Royal Navy on 31 January and then joined the RAF at Cranwell on 1 February 1999. The start of a new era for me, from dark blue to light blue, matelot to crab (as the RAF are called in the other two services). It was ironic really, my father had been in the RN during the Second World War as a seaman; when he left he worked in Nottingham until 1957, then joined the RAF as a motor mechanic. He eventually left the RAF as a sergeant in the mid-1980s and worked for Boots in Nottingham. I was almost following in his footsteps – though I wasn't sure if that was a good thing!

I arrived at Cranwell and started my joining routine, which consisted of signing on the dotted line and pledging allegiance to the Queen again, and then drawing my new uniform, then I learnt how to salute the RAF way and how to come to a halt when marching (the RAF do both like the Army, not the Navy).

That was all done in the tea bar (not the coffee boat as in the Navy), I could see the changes in terminology already. The routine was pretty relaxed though and by Wednesday afternoon I was going back to Yeovilton for the weekend. I returned to Cranwell on Monday to do the Advanced Management Course, which is the same as the Divisional Officers' Course in the RN, and as I had been a Divisional Officer for the last five years, it was not too demanding. After that I went straight to RAF Shawbury to do my RAF 'crab speak' course. The words used in voice marshalling by an aircrewman/loadmaster in a helicopter, are slightly different from in the Navy. Due to my early arrival at Shawbury, 60 Squadron could not employ me for three months, so I ended up on 705 Naval Air Squadron teaching Basic Flying Course students on navigation, before they started Operational Flying Training (OFT) in the Navy. After doing some ground school for the Griffin I completed my RAF voice marshalling course, then I was employed as staff on 60 Squadron until my move onto Chinook helicopters at RAF Odiham.

I joined 27 Squadron to start my Operational Conversion Flight (OCF) at the beginning of July 1999. There were three new Loadmasters on the course with me: Sergeants Jace Hollingsworth, 'Coops' Cooper and Mick Fry, they had just come from the basic course at Shawbury. We started ground school and then flying at the beginning of August. Most of the instructors I had known before and one I knew well: Bob Clements, he had been on the one and only Chinook that was airborne when *Atlantic Conveyor* had been sunk in the Falklands. I knew him from there, but also from the Beirut deployment in 1983/4.

I already had achieved 400 hours flying in the Chinook from my time at Boscombe Down in the 1980s, the course was not too difficult and I was able to help my three fellow students out when it became a little tense for them. We all passed the course. I then went to A flight on 27 Squadron, which was the operational flight, Mick and Jace followed me there and Coops went to 18 Squadron across the other side of the airfield.

CHAPTER 13

The course had lasted six months and at the end I was glad to finish. At the age of nearly 47, being a student again was difficult to accept, but you just have to bite your tongue and grin and bear it! Put lots of effort in and you get the rewards.

While we were on course, the Kosovo operation took place. This was the first operation that I had missed in years, but there was time for more to come, I was sure of that. After Christmas leave, we were off to Norway and Fagernes again, I would be taught how to fly in the Arctic and all about survival. I might have done that before... but at least the skiing was good.

Chapter 14

The next couple of months were taken up gaining my Competency Qualification, which involved doing everything the Chinook was capable of doing: triple hook loads, internal loads, gunning with the minigun (which was awesome – 4,000 rounds of 7.62mm a minute), troop moves and winching; all this both day and night.

At the beginning of May it was planned that two Chinooks from 27 Squadron would embark on HMS *Ocean* for a month's deployment. We had prepped the aircraft and were just about to leave RAF Odiham when the station commander told us to stop. A new plan was formed and we were told that we had to go to Sierra Leone. Another plan was formulated, more internal fuel tanks put in the Chinooks and we were briefed. An hour later we took off and headed for Porto in Portugal; after refuelling we went to Faro in Southern Portugal, then on to Tenerife. Almost an 850-mile sea transit from Faro to Tenerife, then a short stop for food and refuel, before taking off for Dakar in Senegal; another re-fuel and finally to Freetown in Sierra Leone. All in all, it was twenty-four hours of flying in a day-and-a-half. The Americans were astonished that we had achieved the transit from Odiham to Freetown in such a short time with no unserviceabilities.

On arrival at Lungi airfield in Sierra Leone, there was no accommodation or supplies. I had my 'go kit' which I always carried, this included a sleeping bag, bivouac, peak stove cooker and other survival bits and bobs. Most of the RAF crews had come quite ill prepared, as their training did not really cover living rough in the field. We camped by the side of the jungle and started our operational flying with the Parachute Regiment first, and then the Royal Marines when HMS *Ocean* arrived after about five days. There was no fresh water, so everything was bottled; no washing water, so when it rained (and boy did it rain!) we ran out and had a shower. We had to make sure we rinsed the soap off before it stopped pouring down, or else we were left covered in soap suds and only dirty water to rinse off with.

CHAPTER 14

Eventually we moved into the departure lounge of the airport, things were a little more comfortable there, but the heat was constant at about 35°C day and night, quite unbearable at times. It was then that the press started to arrive for a look around; the first to arrive was my old mate Wombat Wooldridge, who was still serving but also working for British Forces Broadcasting Service (BFBS); and then, you guessed it, Kate Adie. She always seemed to turn up when I was on an operation, she must have liked me an awful lot.…

The operation was hot and sweaty, but OK; the children were the most pitiful things. The local thugs had gone around and mutilated most of them, chopping off either their hands or feet. It was a sorry sight, but as the RSM of the detachment, I had to stop the lads feeding these children, as more and more were gathering around our compound. I had to set up a feeding station at the other end of the airfield, where a locally employed worker was used to distribute any left-over rations from our packs. It seemed to work, the children got some food and they were kept way from our compound. I felt like I was being hard on them, but it was for the best. We would have been overrun by hundreds of children asking for help and food.

As for the flying, each morning we would transit down the beach to the west of the airfield and do a test firing of the minigun; we would fire about 1,000 rounds into the sand, just to let the locals know what firepower we had on board. On one occasion we had to land and pick up two lads who had been detained by a patrol of Nigerian UN troops; the lads had gone along a road, killed two men and then been arrested. We landed just up the road from where the two men had been killed. Sergeant Chris 'Splash' Ashton the No.2 crewman, who was at the back of the Chinook, was on his way out to talk to the Nigerian troops when I asked if he was OK with the bodies in the road, he gave thumbs up; some folks are a bit uncertain around dead bodies for the first time. When we got the boys in – and they were definitely boys, one was about 9 and the other about 11 years old – we secured them in the back of the aircraft. The Nigerian troops told us the boys had shot the two men and then approached the troops with AK47s and grenades. The lads then gave themselves up, obviously wanting to get away from whoever was controlling them. What a sorry state to be in.

HMS *Ocean* was now just off the coast of Sierra Leone about five miles out to sea. 846 with Mk4 Sea Kings were embarked and operating alongside us.

One day a task was given to us, which the Sea Kings had been unable to accomplish. HMS *Ocean* wanted a JCB lifted off the back end of the flight deck and taken ashore. It weighed 10.5 tonnes and was only just within the margin for a Chinook to lift. It needed to be at the coolest temperature of the day for us to achieve the lift and with the minimum fuel load on board. We arrived at 0730 off the port quarter of HMS *Ocean*. The load was ready and I was the No.1 crewman at the front of the cabin. We came to a hover over the load, hooked it on and were just about to lift when I stopped the aircraft lifting and told flyco (the flight deck controller) to get the marshaller out of the way, otherwise he would be blown overboard with our downwash. When he had moved, we started to lift the JCB and sure enough, anything that wasn't tied down flew over the side of the ship. The downwash of this now 22,000kg aircraft was tremendous and something to behold.

Later we embarked on HMS *Ocean* and at last got a chance to have a real shower and some decent hot food, plus a few beers. We would still go inland, do tasking and visit the UN Main HQ in a hotel in Freetown. The hotel had a pool and I went for a dip one afternoon and ended up in the presence of Kate Adie again. She gets everywhere!

The last notable event happened just before we left to go back to the UK. HMS *Illustrious* had arrived, with her Sea Harriers embarked. We lifted a spare engine out to them and then shut down on deck, when one of the deck crew came up to me. It was Paul Massey, he had been a young mechanic on 846 with me in the 1980s and was now a lieutenant. We had been on the Westlant deployment in 1981 and the Falklands War together and now he was the flight deck officer on *Illustrious*.

Wing Commander Karl Dixon, the pilot of the aircraft and CO of the squadron, had been to talk to the captain and when he returned, he asked if we would do a demo firing of the minigun for the ship's company and did we have sufficient spare rounds. I said 'yes' and 'yes'. The ship needed to be in a port turn so that we could fire and keep the ship's company safe and also give them the best view. The captain arranged for the ship to be ready and broadcast to the ship's company what would happen.

The target would be the splash target that the Harriers use for practice bombing. They never hit it, they might get close, but it's quite a small piece of metal towed about 500 yards behind the ship to give a water spout as a target.

We launched and I prepped the minigun, I would fire all 4,000 rounds and then reload for the return trip to Lungi. The ship started a port turn, the skipper of *Illustrious* was in the back with me and I got permission to open fire from Karl. When I opened fire, the shockwave and noise was astonishing and at first, I think the skipper was taken aback. But I continued to fire. The water was boiling with lead around the target. I then stopped and asked if the captain wanted a go. He jumped at the chance. He fired about 500 rounds and I could see the horns coming out of his head – he loved it. I then took over again and this time we went slightly closer and I destroyed the splash target, there was nothing left of it when we had finished. After that we dropped the skipper off; he thanked us and declared that it was 'awesome'. It is a fantastic weapon as long as it's maintained properly and does not jam.

Coming from the Navy, I thought there was a slight problem with leadership experience in the RAF. Pilots finish RAF Cranwell, where they do some leadership training, but after that, they have no more visibility of leadership, other than what they see from within their squadrons. During this operation in Sierra Leone this became obvious. The boss had gone home and left the flight commander in charge. The flight commander was a really nice guy, but lacked insight and leadership qualities. Two weeks into the operation the young pilots, as a group, spoke to me of their concerns about the lack of communication and leadership from the flight commander. They didn't know where they stood and lacked confidence in anything they were being told. They asked if I would have a word. I suggested they talked to him, but they thought it would be better coming from me.

I spoke with Jonny and tried to be as diplomatic as possible, explaining about leadership and communication with his subordinates and what it was like when he was a squadron 'Joe'. He took it on the chin and I must admit that things improved from that point onwards.

A couple of weeks later, we set sail in HMS *Ocean* for the UK, job done in Sierra Leone for the present. Just south of the Canary Isles we flew off and transited to Portugal; spent the night in Porto and then back to Odiham for some well-earned leave.

During summer leave Cath and I went to France camping and then home for the last week. Kieran was now a Lieutenant in the Artillery, he had done a tour on 22 Reg Royal Artillery (RA), a Rapier Battery, and was now a troop officer at the Army college in Harrogate. On returning to Odiham, I discovered that a week later I was going to Bosnia again. The task was the same, but this time I was obviously in Chinooks. 845 were still there and the task up at Sipovo was shared between them and us.

The trip lasted until the end of September, but before we left a call came in for us to go down to Dubrovnik. There was a vast grass fire that was threatening the town and we had the capability to lift a Bambi Bucket, for firefighting. The bucket is dunked into the sea, filled up with sea water and the water is then dumped on the fire. We flew down the coast and started putting the fires out. The sortie lasted over five hours; it was hot work, but we felt we were doing a good job. When we got back to Divulje Barracks there was a message from the Dubrovnik authorities saying thank you for a job well done.

In early 2001 we made regular trips to Northern Ireland, as we were dismantling the towers along the border with Southern Ireland. This consisted of lifting 10 tonne containers from the border and taking them back to Bessbrook for removal by lorry. There were a couple of trips up to Scotland and some combat ready tests, plus sea navigation exercises for the new crews who had joined the previous year. The boss called me in at the beginning of April and said I had been chosen to attend the Qualified Helicopter Tactic Instructor Course (QHTI) which started in May. The course consisted of a three week ground phase based at RAF Benson and then a three week flying phase based at RAF Leuchars in Scotland.

I had to do a fair amount of studying before the course started, as the exam at the opening of the course was quite high level. There were a few visits to military and civilian arms manufactures and operators, and lectures from companies and high ranking officers about future developments and tactics which were very interesting. Then I was asked to deliver a half hour presentation on a subject that linked in with the QHTI Course. I pondered for about two seconds then decided on the incident in the Falklands when we had been attacked by A4 Skyhawks. I went to the Fleet Air Arm Museum and took a photograph of the section of our blade with the 20mm cannon hole through and produced my presentation on power point.

I delivered the presentation and ended by saying it was all about the trust between pilot and crew. If Simon Thornewill had not broken to the left when I shouted 'break left', the crew would have died. He did that without hesitation and we survived. The audience was silent and then a few questions were asked about the incident. They had not heard the story before and a few students asked if they could have my presentation. Then the CO of the course asked if he could retain my presentation, stating that I had been the only student ever to come through on the course who had actually carried out fighter evasion for real.

The ground phase finished after a number of simulation sorties and we moved up to Leuchars. The flying phase consisted of electronic warfare instruction and evasion, fighter evasion, helicopter verses helicopter evasion and then ended in a tactical warfare exercise involving all the resources available, both ground and air. The flying phase was excellent; it was a series of high energy sorties and not for anyone who suffered from airsickness. Being attacked by fixed-wing fighters and helicopters over a three-hour sortie, being able to navigate and continue on a pre-ordained task and achieve that task was what it was all about. By the end of the course, I had instructed students on all of these procedures, debriefed and written them up in a report.

I passed the course and was now a qualified QHTI, A2 QAI. More responsibility but no more money, which was a bit of a bummer.

I left RAF Leuchars and went on leave to return to RAF Odiham at the beginning of August. A nice break again, after being away for six weeks.

The rest of the year included a lot of gunning, using the M134 (Minigun) and M60 single-barrelled machine gun, plus displays and trips over to NI again to complete the container lifts out of South Armagh.

In November it was back up to Leuchars in Scotland, but this time on a major exercise with similar content to the QHTI course, although involving many more assets and troops. The best thing, though, was because there was no accommodation at RAF Leuchars, we had to live in the Old Course Hotel in St Andrews; unfortunately, we didn't get to play golf on the old course while we were there. Maybe one day.

Chapter 15

We started 2002 with a detachment to Norway, back in the snow again; a bit different from all the warmer Mediterranean and African trips I had been on recently. We were in Fagernes until the end of March, completing survival training and requalifying in Arctic operations. Once again the skiing was good, apart from one of the pilots breaking his lower leg while skiing on snow blades, which are very short skis.

I was back home again for Easter leave and Cath and I were planning to go to the 25th anniversary celebrations of the ACA, an association for Royal Navy aircrewmen, past and present, established in 1977 by a small band of aircrewmen in a pub in Portland; it now has a membership of over 450. Two days before the ACA 25th, I got a phone call from the Commanding Officer of 27 squadron, Wing Commander Shaun Reynolds. The squadron was to deploy a flight to Afghanistan, in support of 45 Commando Royal Marines, who had been sent out to help the American Forces around the Pakistan border. The boss explained I was to go and would deploy out of Brize Norton in thirty-six hours. Deep joy. But… life in a blue suit, light blue now, not dark blue, but blue all the same.

So, I packed again for another operation, with my weapons, go kit, flying gear, bed, sleeping bag and personal gear, like sports kit and music, can't forget your music, can you? Two days later I was in a tent at the American airfield in Bagram, Northern Afghanistan. A day later the aircraft arrived and were rebuilt ready for operations between Kabul, the capital, and the Pakistan border near Kowst airfield, which had been run by the Russians when they had invaded the country years before.

The weather was not quite what I expected. It was still cold, in fact at night the temperature was down to about minus 4°C and up to 20°C during the day. Bagram was at 7,000ft above sea level, so altitude also came in to play. The airfield was mined all around the taxiways and runways, so no going off piste here, stay on the hard standings or there was the strong possibility of being blown up.

The flying started at pace, down to the border or into Kabul. The M134 and M60 were tested on each flight, as we needed to be confident that our weapons worked. Tasking was around the high ground from the Hindu Cush past the Khyber Pass and down to Kowst. We were inserting Royal Marines from 45 Commando onto the peaks of mountains up to 13,000ft; initially we had no oxygen, but later the aircraft were modified to provide that facility.

The longer the operation went on the hotter it got, so that by the time May came around, we were working in temperatures of around plus 45°C, and that was up at 5,000ft. The tasks sometimes involved inserting twenty troops on top of ridges, where there was no landing site. We would place the back wheels of the aircraft on the ridge, or pinnacle, with the rest of the Chinook hanging in the air, lower the ramp and get the lads off as soon as we could. On one occasion we were doing this and there was a 1,000ft drop just off the back of the ramp, one Marine leapt out, let go of his kit and it went straight down the cliff face, not sure if he ever got it back.

The heavy flying programme continued, we got shot at quite a few times, holes in the blades and fuselage, only from an AK47 but still enough to ruin your day if you got hit. The tasks came in thick and fast, all sorts of jobs from various units, black and green forces and different nationalities. One operation was due to go in before dawn, it was as dark as night could be. This was a formation of two of our Chinooks and two American aircraft. The boss was flying and I was the lead crewman, the route was through the mountain ranges, and not an easy route at that. We had no infrared facility and it was starting to get dangerous even on NVG, because the light levels were so poor. The left-hand seat pilot wanted to push on, but the boss asked me as the QHTI if we should. I said the better part of valour would be to go back, wait until the light levels got better and then come back at first light, it was better than losing an aircraft in these conditions. He agreed with me, so we turned around and made our way back to the low ground and waited until daybreak, then set off again to complete the insertion with no issues or losses. That day we completed some ten hours flying, but we were away from our base for sixteen hours. A long night and day!

On 12 June we had flown down to Kowst to do a troop insert; when we landed on our return there was a reception party, the boss was there with a bottle of champagne (not sure where he got it, as everyone was dry). I had just cracked my 7,000 hours flying in helicopters. We had a drink and a photograph and then as I was walking back, the crewmen came out with foam fire extinguishers and proceeded to cover me with foam from head to toe. A nice reception I thought!

The RAF flying order rules stipulate that you are only allowed to fly a maximum of 250 hours in any three-month period; I had kept it quiet, but someone saw the details and I was grounded for a week because I had flown over 260 hours in just over eighty days while in Afghanistan.

Our part of the operation was concluding, but there had been a few tragic incidents during our stay at Bagram. A girl had tried to come up close to the perimeter fence and stood on a mine, she died instantly. There had also been an attempted attack on the base by a group of men the week before, so it was never safe there. One benefit was that we were at altitude and each day when we weren't flying, Splash, Craig Wadeson, me and a couple of others used to run around the taxiway (not mined). We were not drinking alcohol and I had lost about a stone-and-a-half. This meant that we were getting extremely fit and as all this training was at altitude, that really helped our cardiac fitness.

We decided to do a charity run from Bagram to Kabul, some forty-two miles. It was planned for us do it as a relay, with two runners doing about two miles each leg. At the start the temperature was about 40°C, but it was getting hotter and hotter as we got closer and closer to Kabul. All along the route we had armoured cover by a section of troops and also a Chinook in the air, we achieved the run and raised quite a lot for the squadron charity.

By the time I left Afghanistan I had flown another seventy hours. I would have stayed until the detachment ended, but as Kieran and his partner Naomi were due to get married in July I managed to get away a week early. There was no way I was going to miss my son's wedding, I had been away for a lot of Kieran's life, but this was one occasion that I did not want to miss.

Kieran and Naomi's wedding turned out to be a great day, the weather and the occasion was perfect. The wedding was at Naomi's parents' local church in Cornwall and the reception at St Mellion Golf Club near Plymouth.

Kieran was dressed in his uniform and Naomi looked beautiful in her wedding dress. As they came into the golf club, arm in arm, an old lady at the entrance said, 'You do look beautiful, dear.' Naomi thanked her and the old lady said, 'Not you love, him.' A fantastic day though, and many a pint or Pimm's drunk that night.

I had been on 27 Squadron for three years and I knew change would come soon and sure enough, when I got back after summer leave I got the call that I was to move on. I had put in for the Cyprus SAR Flight or the C17 job at Brize Norton; I knew I wouldn't get them. My last choice – but really my first – was to go back to RWTS at Boscombe Down, this time as the RAF Master Loadmaster. I saw the boss and he told me I was to move to RWTS at the beginning of September. He thanked me for my efforts while I was on 27 Squadron and said I had done a fantastic job, both on operations and as the flight master. Thankfully my write ups also reflected that.

So, another new era in my career was about to begin. I was happy with this new appointment especially as the boss was a certain Commander Steve Daniels, the senior pilot was Roger Moffatt, who lived next door to me in Yeovilton, and the Naval Chief Aircrewmen was John Fagan (Fagbin/Fags), who I had known for some considerable time. I was very happy with that! I also had an easier commute home each day as it was only fifty miles down the A303, rather than ninety miles down the A303 and M3.

Joining Rotary Wing Test Squadron again was like going back to the Navy, the Boss, SP and four other Naval test pilots were there, four Army test pilots and four RAF test pilots, plus of course John Fagan; these where a good bunch of men and I knew most of them quite well. On joining the squadron, I went down to see the engineers and flight test observers/engineers, several of them were still there from when I left the squadron in 1988. It really was like coming home, even though it was fourteen years later.

My career at RWTS began with me getting a couple of medals. I had already got the Sierra Leone Medal on 27 Squadron, but not the Afghanistan medal, plus I was also to get a bar to my Long Service Medal (LSGC). This one was quite rare, as it was an RAF bar to a Royal Navy Long Service Medal – there aren't many of those around! This meant that I now had nine medals, with a bar to my LSGC and a bar to the General Service Medal. It was costing a fortune each time I got a new medal as they had to be remounted, but hey-ho a big chest full now.

The flying on RWTS started immediately, first on the Merlin, which I had done trials for in the 1980s, but it was now in service with the Navy (Mk1) and RAF (Mk3). I completed some ground school and simulator training and then got left-hand seat qualified. At Boscombe there were also six Mk3 Chinooks; a fat tank version of the Mk2 but with different flight instruments and flight control systems. I had a quick conversion and was qualified to operate the Mk3.

It was like old times, qualified now in all types of helicopter from Gazelle to Chinook and all military types of helicopter in between. Like before on RWTS, the flying was very varied from trials, doing first of class to new equipment and flight system trials, to clearance of Special Forces flight trials and procedures. This included cutting edge trials and long distance radio operations and communication systems testing.

The Merlin and Chinook Mk3 clearances gathered pace as the front line needed these capabilities as soon as possible, we were doing all manner of trials: sloping ground, ramp loading and gunnery, external loads, winching, performance, heavy machine gunnery, FLIR (infra-red), NVG and hot and high trials. One of the more exciting trials was for the new engines fitted to the Chinook Mk3, at 15,000ft, on oxygen and wearing parachutes, doing engine shut downs, restarts and performance checks at height.

During our time at RWTS, Fags and I would try to play squash as much as possible, we had played a few times before. I am quite handy at racquet sports, but Fags, maybe not to the same level. Anyway, we still play even now and at present after 20 years he has still only beaten me twice, how he maintains his enthusiasm to keep competing amazes me; but he does and we still enjoy playing and competing against each other in all manner of sports.

The rest of the year was taken up by a series of interesting sorties and training flights. The main emphasis was on preparing to go to the USA for the performance trial in the Sea King. It would take place in Wyoming, California and Arizona. The trial was to gather performance data, to confirm that all the new data graphs that had been produced for plastic blades on the Sea King were correct and if they were not, to rewrite all the data. Most of these flights would either be at altitude or tethered hovering, which meant that we were attached to the earth by a cable, either 10ft long or 100ft long. During tethered hovering we would lift to the hover and then pull as much power as is required. It can be quite a dodgy procedure though, as the trial must be flown to the letter and a certain technique followed. The communication between the crewman, pilot and ground crew was essential.

On one occasion at Boscombe Down this communication broke down, there was no crewman required in the aircraft at the time and the flight was directed by the ground crew. On completion of the sortie the pilot thought the tether cable had been released from the hook on the underside of the Sea King, it had not; the pilot transitioned away for a refuel and as he did so the cable pulled him into the ground. The crew managed to get out of the aircraft but it was destroyed by fire. A very serious incident. After a review of the techniques the crew composition was changed to always include flying with a crewman on board in the back of the aircraft, for positioning, clearances and confirmation that the tether cable was released from the load-lifting hook, before departing the operating site.

CHAPTER 15

On gathering a lot of data, a graph of performance versus altitude, weight, speed and temperature could be written. This was what the boffins where there to do! So, we practised the procedures and technique at Boscombe Down before we left for the States at the beginning of January 2005.

We were to get a British Airways flight to Denver, but unfortunately the travel arrangements had been booked a little late and we were all put into cattle class, not 'traveller plus' as promised. The leg room was short and as most of us were 6ft plus the long flight was awful; because of that we ended up standing at the back of the cabin, next to the bar/stewardess area chatting and drinking for almost the entire flight. In Denver we went out for a meal and drink; it was my birthday, so I had to have some celebration after a long day in the air.

The next day we left Denver for Pinedale in Wyoming, via Rock Springs. It was winter and very cold in Wyoming, plus the trial site was at 7,000ft, which was the reason for going there. The hotel in Pinedale was nice and the small airfield was perfect for the purpose of the trial.

I had gone out with the boss, Steve Daniels and Tim Eldridge a Navy Lieutenant, a good crew to go out with. Fags and Steve had delivered the aircraft to Pinedale just before Christmas, so it was there waiting for us to start the flying trials.

Steve, Tim and I briefed the first morning to go flying and do a quick check test flight. On manning up there was a problem with the engine system, so we shut down for the engineers to investigate. Eventually, after three days we got airborne and managed nine trials' sorties before the problem manifested itself again – in a big way. The aircraft was unserviceable and out of action for a period of nine days. We couldn't do any trials work, so we went skiing in the Teton mountains from the resort of Jackson Hole, about thirty-five miles north of Pinedale; one of the best ski resorts in the world. An area pass was $75 per day, so I asked about military discount and was told we would be charged just $30 per day. All those who were with me were also entitled to the reduced fee – the civvies were happy with that! I love the way the Americans treat their military. We spent the next three days skiing, a winner in my eyes and what a fantastic place to ski!

We had settled in with the locals by now and frequented the Wind River micro-brewery and grill in Pinedale, the beer and food were OK. Eating out all the time eventually became a bit of a pain though; American food is good, but they never seem to have vegetables with the meal. In the end we started taking vitamin supplements to keep up our strength.

It was coming up to Burns Night at the end of January; Steve ordered some haggis and had them flown out from Scotland, and we had booked a restaurant called the Old Stones for the night. A few of us got dressed up. I had managed to get a tartan table cloth as a kilt and we celebrated Burns night. It was good, but the locals thought we were mad, killing a Haggis and reciting an old Scottish verse called the 'Address to the Haggis'. After we had all eaten and performed the Burns Night ritual we went across to the cowboy bar, which was full of local red necks. It was −18°C outside and when we walked in from the cold, the red necks couldn't believe their eyes. A load of Brits had just come in dressed in skirts, with silly hats on and wanted whisky, not bourbon to drink. They soon joined in with us and we had quite a good night.

Next morning back to work again, the aircraft had been repaired and so we started more intense test flying and tethered hovering. The temperature was now about -23°C and the recirculation of the cold wind, snow and downdraft was tremendous. It was so cold in the back with the door open that I was wearing extra gloves, plus a face mask and Arctic jacket. We flew for about two hours at a time and then spent another two hours warming up.

The trial had gone quite well, Steve and Tim took turns in flying from the right-hand seat, I was always in the back and we now had the routine down to a T. We could climb with the 100ft tether and I would voice marshal the aircraft up as we took the weight, I would count down the height to climb in feet, 10 ft, 8 ft, 6 ft, 5, 4, 3, 2, 1, and the weight would come on. It was almost telepathy the way we did it. Perfection; well we thought so! And the trials officers were always impressed.

Eventually we had completed all of the test points at Pinedale and Big Piney, another small airfield about ten miles from Pinedale. The whole detachment prepared to fly down to Pendleton, a US Marine Corps airfield on the Californian Coast between San Diego and Los Angeles. Most of the engineers would fly down to California by passenger aircraft, but five of us flew down in the Sea King. This was going to be a once in a lifetime trip, to be able to fly in a helicopter down from Wyoming, south via the Green and Colorado rivers, through Lake Powel into the Grand Canyon, Las Vegas and then on to California.

I planned the trip, it would take two long days of flying. On the first day we planned to fly from Pinedale to Las Vegas, and the following day down through the Mojave Desert and on to Pendleton. That was the plan anyway.

We set off and the weather was appalling, with snow, low cloud and high winds, we grovelled down to Rock Springs at about 100ft and then down the river to Vernal in Utah. The weather got worse and Steve and I started using our ultra-low-level navigation skills to find our way to the airfield in Vernal flying sometimes down to about 50ft, a couple of times slowing almost to a hover; we popped out of a valley, under some 200ft power cables and found the runway. A two-hour delay and a stopover at Vernal. The weather eventually improved, so we planned the next leg and set off for Vegas via Lake Powel and Page.

We set off at about 500ft and, as forecast, the viability had improved immensely, so much so that when we got further south and were over the plain north of Lake Powel, I pointed out a Butte to Steve who was flying at the time. I wanted him to pass two miles to the right of the Butte. When I told him this it was 110 miles to the Butte, he was astonished, the visibility was so good we could see for well over 130 miles.

As we went down the river to Lake Powel the scenery was outstanding; cliffs, river rapids and lots of holiday sites along the waterway, a real out-of-the-way holiday resort. It was then that we had a slight problem, a warning caption lit up. It was a generator failure. We went through the emergency procedure in the flight reference cards and tried to reset it, the generator would not reset, so we made for the closest airfield which was at Lake Powel. The two engineers who had travelled with us, John and Dave, looked at the fault when we landed, but without a spare generator they could not fix the problem. After a phone call, we booked a hotel and put the aircraft to bed for the night. The spares should arrive the next day, all being well!

The spares arrived the next day by courier and by mid-afternoon, and after a ground run, the problem had been fixed. We submitted the flight plan and set off for Las Vegas. To get there we had to transit along the northern edge of the Grand Canyon. The sight was awesome, until you see it for real you cannot comprehend how big the Grand Canyon actually is. The next event was to land at the Las Vegas North airfield, having transited the northern edge of Vegas itself.

I had not pre-booked a hotel, so I got on the phone. The company QINETIQ were paying so I thought I might as well go big. I phoned the Miramar Hotel on the Strip and asked how much the rooms were. Dave had the credit card so I relayed to him that the only rooms available were five penthouse suites and that they were $299 each. He agreed and I booked them. A little white lie… but we deserved good rooms for the night – and they were incredible: suites with a full en-suite shower, bath and jacuzzi, plus a TV in the end of the bed and a full bar. Happy days.

The next morning, we took off around 9am and flew across the Mojave Desert towards California, passing over Palm Springs, Mount San Jacinto and arriving into USMC Pendleton on the afternoon of 17 February where the next part of the trial would take place. That was to be the end of our flying for a while because as we made our approach to the USMC base the electrical problem we had experienced previously at Pinedale occurred again, we were short finals for the airfield, landed the aircraft, taxied in and shut the Sea King down and we left it to the engineers who had flown down from Wyoming by civilian airline. Our relief crew flew out a week later to let us return to the UK, Fags was my relief.

One of the flight test engineer trials officers and I had driven up from Carlsbad to pick up Fags and Flight Lieutenant Phil Merritt, who had flown in from Heathrow together. As you might know, a 'fag' in America means something quite different than in the UK, so I decided to give Fags and Phil a laugh after their long journey. I thought that if I made a sign for when Fags entered Arrivals, it would make him chuckle. I wrote FAGS in big letters with a marker pen across a large piece of card. As Phil and Fags entered arrivals I held up the card, waved to them effeminately, ran up to Fags and gave him a big kiss and a hug. Fags saw the funny side, but the waiting crowd were a little startled – or thought we were mad Brits. The trials officer didn't know where to put his face and I think it embarrassed him slightly. Military humour, eh?

Three days later after a few nights out with the new crew, Steve and I were driven up to Long Beach for the night, before flying back the next day to Heathrow. Fags had a whale of a time because the aircraft was downbird/broken for a couple of weeks more, so he got to spend the next fourteen days around the pool at the hotel. The engineers had to change the main loom which led from the fuel computers up to the engines. This was a considerable and complicated job, as the engines had to be lifted up while the loom was changed.

On 25 February after an overnight flight from LA I got home to Yeovilton, I suffered jetlag for a while, but recovered after a couple of days, it's always worst going from West to East I think? While I had been away, Naomi and Kieran announced that Naomi would be giving birth to our first grandchild around June 2005. A grandad at only 52, quite young I thought, but still very nice.

I returned to the States on 4 May. I should have gone to Arizona to replace Fags again on the trial as the aircraft was planned to move to Phoenix after a month of trials in California. In the event, the aircraft took a considerable time to get fixed and so the trial was to stay in California, so I found myself heading back to LAX. Phil Merritt picked me up, but no posters or kisses this time.

Fags had gone flying around the Grand Canyon with a trials officer who had rented a light aircraft. Unfortunately, as they took off from the Grand Canyon airfield, which was at 6,000ft, they had a slight engine problem. As they lifted the wheels came up, the engine power decreased, and they ran out of available runway. They crashed between two trees, but luckily they all survived with only a few scratches and were released from hospital a few hours later and made their way back to our hotel in Carlsbad.

I woke early next morning, with my body clock still on UK time. I checked on Fags in his room; he was OK, just a bit shaken, so I suggested we go for a run along the beach to help ease his mind and body. Later that day we cleared all the remaining cobwebs and thoughts about the accident away during a really good night out at an Irish bar. Two days later I put him on a plane back to Heathrow, warning him he might have to come back out again to relieve me up in Wyoming for the next stage of the trial. Simon was getting married to his fiancée Michelle in August and I had no intention of missing their wedding if the trials dragged on.

On 4 June I got the phone call from Kieran that I had been waiting for: Naomi had given birth to a little boy, his name was Benjamin (Ben) and I was now a grandad.

Tim Eldridge was still at Pendleton with me, but now another test pilot called Lieutenant Commander Mark 'Sparky' Macleod had taken over from Phil Merritt. The aircraft had been repaired and we started flying lots of hours, the majority of which was still tethered hovering, with a little load lifting and some low-level performance trials.

We stayed at Pendleton until 5 June, when we returned north to Pinedale in Wyoming. This time though, with the daylight lasting longer, it was to be a one-day trip. That amazing trip south which I thought would be once in a lifetime, I was lucky enough to do again in the opposite direction. Being the reverse route there were a couple of minor changes, but it was still a fantastic experience. People pay thousands to see the views along that route and I had the pleasure of flying it twice.

The trials continued at pace during the week, and we were kept busy. We did have some time off and manged to visit Yellowstone Park where we saw Old Faithful, the large super-heated water geyser which goes off every thirty minutes, plus some bears (at a distance) and eagles nesting in very tall tree tops. Even in June though, it still managed to snow on us.

Sparky Macleod went home and Lieutenant Commander Steve Jose came out to replace him and we continued tethered hovering and low-speed performance flying. We moved up to Idaho for a couple of days to continue flying when increasing winds caused problems. My last flight in Pinedale was on 23 July. Fags was going to replace me, so I could go home for Simon and Michelle's wedding in Warminster. I got home the next day and after a few hours' sleep went to see our new grandson. Kieran had made it back from Iraq for two weeks RNR to be at the birth. Fortunately, his tour was completed by the day of his brother's wedding.

After summer leave and a great holiday with Cath in our camper in France, I returned to more test flying, everything from Gazelle to Chinook. It was great to be flying in so many types of aircraft. Steve Daniels was to leave the squadron the month I returned to Boscombe, he was to be promoted Captain, which he really deserved. The new boss was Lieutenant Colonel Ian Burton from the AAC. Steve Daniels was a hard act to follow and coming from the Army, Ian Burton had a different perspective on leadership compared to most other people I had worked with on RWTS, he was more Army orientated, which was good in some respects, but in my opinion he was never going to fill Steve's shoes.

Later that year there was an opportunity to attend an NVG conference in Baltimore. I volunteered to attend, along with Fags and Steve Jose; we had volunteered before but were never selected so our flabber was gasted when all three of us were given the nod that we would be able to attend. The main conference arena was in the centre of the Baltimore, down by the waterfront. The city was lovely but the conference was dull. Instead of presenting cutting-edge technology, the presenters for the companies were just putting forward a sales pitch. As members of a test flight squadron, we had worked with the latest equipment, so didn't need the sales push. We spent the first day of the three-day conference at the arena, but decided that if the second day was as dull as the first, Fags and I would leave early. Steve wanted to stay for a certain presentation that took place later on in the morning.

The first speaker stood up and yes, it was another sales pitch; Fags and I told Steve we were going to the harbourside for a coffee, again Steve said he would stay. As we were walking to the waterfront a few minutes later we heard the patter of tiny feet as Steve came running up behind us – he had also given up. We decided to make a move so packed up and drove to Washington. We saw the sites around Capitol Hill and the White House, plus all the normal sites like the Lincoln Memorial, the Iwo Jima Monument and Arlington Cemetery, which was quite moving.

CHAPTER 15

The next few months were taken up with two big Chinook trials, examining performance and controls systems for the Mk2 aircraft, this involved flying in a lot of different conditions. Long and short duration flights and back to some of my favourite flying, tethered hovering, deep joy! A load-lifting trial was next, using single-use lift bags (SULB) these were disposable bags that could hold two tonnes of stores each, or loads that we just drop off to the troops, and the bags don't need to be recovered. A much speedier technique, especially when load lifting into a hot/active landing Zone, i.e. someone is shooting at you! The system worked well and was employed in Afghanistan very quickly after we had trialled it.

Chapter 16

2006 seemed to come around very quickly, but the year was full of trials at Boscombe with lots of Chinook work, a few Sea King trials and other associated flying trials in military aircraft. The main new piece of equipment we did have to test though, was a new design of Sea King blade (Carson Blades). This blade had a swept-back tip, which gave it better performance at altitude and speed. We tested the blades in the UK, but the following year there would be a full performance trial at Gunnison in Colorado. Fags would start off in Gunnison, then I would go out later to replace him. Kieran was now a Captain in the Artillery and was posted to 4 Regiment RA at Osnabruck in Germany. Simon had settled down to life as a sports teacher at Warminster School in Wiltshire and Cath I think was quite contented. All seemed rosy at the time in the Sheldon family.

2007 started much like 2006, lots of work but mostly around Boscombe Down and Westlands at Yeovil. I had convinced the Commanding Officer of RAF Boscombe Down to give me a shedload of money to take eighteen people away in February on an adventurous training (AT) period, this was a ski trip to Garmisch Partenkirchen in the Bavarian Alps in Germany. We had three ski instructors on the squadron, Dave Marsden, Andy Ozanne and myself. I, along with the help of Fags, would run the event which would be over a ten-day period, driving through France down to Bavaria in two mini buses and qualifying everyone in alpine skiing. The trip was great, good accommodation, food, wine and above all skiing. This was the first AT period we had achieved on the squadron since 2001, so that was a tick in the box and every man and woman who went really enjoyed the period away.

The Carson Blade trial was delayed slightly, so it was not until April that the detachment set out for the Rocky Mountains in Colorado just to the south west of Denver.

With Fags away in the USA from the end of April, I was left to do all the Chinook, Merlin and Sea King flying, of which there was a lot. Our new exchange test pilot at the time was a US Army Warrant Officer called Nolan Beck; he was an excellent pilot and a really nice chap. He had just joined the squadron and wanted to be shown around the south west of England, so I organised a navigation trip for him. We left Boscombe in a Sea King Mk4, just myself and Nolan on board; we flew west to Bristol, up the Wye Valley to RAF Shawbury where we had lunch and refuelled, then went through the Manchester helicopter route and up to my mother-in-law's in Adlington, where we flew past her house, that was nice for her and for Nolan to see the Lancashire skyline to the north of Manchester. We then returned via Chatsworth House, Oxford and finally to Boscombe Down. The whole trip was planned and conducted to give Nolan the best view of the areas he may be flying around in the next four years of his tour.

In August I left to go out to Gunnison and replace Fags on the Carson trial. The airfield at Gunnison was at 8,000ft which gave us all the temperatures and altitude we needed for the performance data gathering. Back to tether hovering at altitude, deep joy! This time, however, it was nice and warm. I was only out in Gunnison for two weeks, we had gathered all the performance data that the boffins required to rewrite the performance graphs for the operators and Westlands to refer to in the future. On returning to Boscombe Down, I arranged to do a navigation sortie with Nolan around London, through the London helicopter routes and across Heathrow. It is a fantastic sight to fly around the capital and even better at night, which I managed to do with Nolan later the next month.

2007 was also a great year for the family. Naomi gave birth to a little girl, Emma, in February and around the same time we found out that Michelle was expecting a child. Ryan was born in October, so we ended the year with three grandchildren!

Chapter 17

2008 was to be my last year in the Services; I had applied for an extension of my contract which was due to expire on 1 January 2008, the day before my 55th birthday. The appointer said he was happy for me to extend my contract, in fact he offered me an extra five years on the proviso that I go back to be the crewman leader of either the Puma Squadron in Ireland, the Merlin Squadron at RAF Benson or back to Chinooks at Odiham, all three units meant working away from home. The Puma unit in Northern Ireland was be based at RAF Aldergrove, this was at Northern Ireland's main airport, the Merlin and Chinook Squadrons were still operating out in Iraq and Afghanistan. I had got the ticks in boxes for all of those places and didn't really want to go back at my age. All I wanted was an extra nine months to take me up to the same breakpoint as Cath, as she would retire in September from the Civil Service and then we could retire together at the end of August 2008. The deal was struck and I would leave on 31 August and stay at RWTS until then, that worked for all of us!

In April we conducted a Chinook trial which involved going up to 17,000ft and carrying out certain high-energy manoeuvres. The trial was done at that height so if anything went wrong, we would have time to bail out; we all had parachutes fitted and were on oxygen. Fortunately I had parachuted before, so had an idea what it would be like, which could not be said for some of the trials officers who were sat on the consoles in the cabin. I think they were a little apprehensive about going so high and the thought of what might happen. Fortunately the trial went ahead OK and we got all the required data, there were a few hairy moments with a series of control problems and engine malfunctions, but nothing that couldn't be put right at the end of the day.

At the beginning of May an urgent trial instruction was received; this was for the Sea King Mk4s from the Navy, who were out in Afghanistan and were feeling a little vulnerable, not having a machine gun on the port (left) side. We were tasked to carry out a short notice port-door gun trial. This involved all the safety requirements and arcs of fire and then shooting the GPMG from different ranges and heights both day and night and on NVG. I was to carry out the firings, which didn't go down too well with the main trials officer, who thought he should do it. That was never going to happen, because he couldn't hit a barn door at ten paces from the air and he didn't have any experience of firing a weapon out of the doorway of a helicopter flying at 100 mph. The trial progressed at speed and the following week the weapon was in use, in the port door, in Afghanistan. Who says the system doesn't work when it needs to?

I was due to leave the squadron at the end of May, allowing for all the leave I was due, including terminal leave and resettlement leave, which took me up to the end of August and my final date in the RAF. At the beginning of May, I had been talking to Major Tim Peake, who was one of our test pilots on RWTS. His main role on the squadron was as an Apache Test Pilot. I said that as the Apache was a two pilot aircraft, Fags and I as aircrewmen never got to fly in the beast. Later that week, Tim came to see me to say he was doing some general handling in the Apache and needed a front seat pilot, and was I up for it. I jumped at the chance.

Tim started the Apache up and gave me control. I taxied it out and took off and the next two hours were mine, flying around Salisbury plain training area. It handled like a dream and only when Tim wanted to show me some attack profiles, did he take over control. As the sortie came to an end we did a flypast at RWTS Boscombe Down, going past the squadron building at low level for a quick photograph, then back to Middle Wallop. I flew in it only once, but it was a great experience. Of course, Tim went on to better things – he went on to be an astronaut and spent six months on the International Space Station.

Before I went on leave for the last time, I volunteered for to go to Russia on a battlefield tour. We were in Moscow for three days with a Russian guide from the British Embassy who showed us Red Square, the Kremlin, Lenin lying in state and all the other sights of interest. It was great having an insider show us around. The fact that we were followed everywhere made no difference, we just had to watch our step, what we did and what we said.

On the fourth day we got a flight down to Volgograd, formally Stalingrad in the Second World War. The flight was interesting; it was in an old Ilyushin bomber which was now a civil airliner. The bomb aimer's glass-fronted spotting dome was still in place and the seats were very basic and loose in their mountings; I doubt they would remain anchored to the floor in the event of a crash. Anyway, the aircraft got us to Volgograd and we started our battlefield tour. First, we saw the vast statue of Mother Russia; standing at 280ft with a sword in one hand, it was erected in 1967 by Vuchetich and Nikitin and dedicated to the heroes of the battle of Stalingrad, most impressive! Some of the old wartime buildings still stand in Volgograd itself which gave an idea of what it was really like during the conflict there. The film *Enemy at the Gates* portrays the battle well and there is still a monument to Vasily Zaitsev, the Russian sniper who shot 225 Germans during the siege.

On leaving Volgograd we returned to Moscow, this time in a Boeing 727, much better I thought. We spent the final night in a hotel by the main Moscow airport. It was a shame we couldn't stay longer, because it was the final of the European Cup the following night between Manchester United and Chelsea, but I could hardly complain; I had been to Russia, which was something I thought I would never be able to do years before, during the Cold War.

The final event of note was Nolan's and my leaving dinner; I was leaving the Service, the squadron and the RAF, and Nolan was leaving the squadron, to return to the States. Fags had organised the Senior Rates Mess on HMS *Victory*, Nelson's flagship, as our dining out venue, what an honour, it was a great occasion and we both loved the send-off.

My last flight in the RAF was with Nolan in one of the Gazelles from ETPS (Empire Test Pilots School), we had it for two hours and went off on a jolly around the south east of England. It was good to see out the end of my RAF flying career with Nolan, he was such a nice man. After the two hours were up we landed at the squadron rather than ETPS, that was a late change organised by the boss. When we touched down and got out of the Gazelle, a group of the squadron aircrew grabbed us both (we knew it would happen), they tied us to a flatbed trailer and then the whole squadron came out, including all the engineers and trials officers and they all proceeded to douse us with very cold water. In the end it was quite a good send off, after all I had been flying now for some thirty-six years and Nolan was on his way over the pond back to the US Army.

Between leaving the RAF and the end of August I had arranged some resettlement courses. This is a programme in the military to prepare servicemen and women for life outside the service. I had chosen to do a three-week property maintenance course in Bristol, doing bricklaying, plumbing, plastering, block paving, and all sorts of jobs that would be

CHAPTER 17

required for property upkeep and maintenance. It was a really good course and taught me a lot of skills that would come into good use later when Kieran and Simon both purchased run-down houses in need of renovation, repair and a lot of hard work.

The second course I managed to arrange was near Barnstaple in Devon, with a man called Mike Watts who taught fine woodworking classes. It would be a three-week long residential course and as I had always enjoyed woodworking, this would give me extra skills on top of the experience I had already gained at school and over the last thirty years of DIY. Mike asked what I wanted to achieve on the course and I explained that I wanted to improve my woodworking skills and techniques and would like to build some classic furniture.

After designing a two-drawer, fine-dovetail hallway table, I was taken aback slightly when Mike presented me with a slice of Ash cut from a tree length about 12ft long, 2ft wide and about 3in thick – and it still had the bark on. Over the next six days, Mike taught me to thickness plane, cut and size the wood for my project. The table turned out really well, and considering that it started off as a plank of Ash and ended up as a hand-crafted piece of furniture, I felt I had achieved a great deal. Cath thought it was great and that really was the highest accolade I could hope for.

I had been in the military for forty years, man and boy, so what next? I asked the Royal Naval Reserve Air Branch if I could join and do some reserve time at Yeovilton, but they said no – I was too old at 56 years of age. I didn't want a full-time job and didn't really need the money as I had my pension and Cath had her state pension, plus a small Civil Service pension so we were financially secure. An offer of a job did come from an aviation firm based at Bournemouth airport, but that was full time so I declined. Cath and I would survive, no mortgage to pay and no children to look after, all was pretty good.

My final day in the RAF came on 31 August 2008. I had achieved a lot in my forty years of service. Starting out as a junior seaman in the Royal Navy I had progressed to Warrant Officer 1, transferred to the RAF and completed my time as a Master Aircrew test flying at Boscombe Down. I had flown every helicopter the British military had operated during those forty years – plus some more; survived all the conflicts I had been sent to, with quite a few near misses, but survived nonetheless. My one regret was that I had not quite hit the milestone of 8,000 flying hours; I was a mere 149 hours short at 7,851, but hey ho!

I was resigned to not having a job for the time being, maybe some part-time employment to subsidise my pension might come along, but until then Cath and I were happy with the way things were. I still went to Yeovilton with John Fagan, as he had now moved from Boscombe Down and was working in the Tasking cell at the Commando Helicopter Force HQ (CHF HQ). We played squash – he was still not winning any games, but maintained his hope of winning one day. Like my 8,000 hours that would probably never happen?

About the same time I left the RAF, Kieran and Naomi bought a house in a village called Shipton Bellinger near Tidworth, which was where Kieran had been posted. Kieran and Naomi loved it, but I wasn't quite so keen; the problem was that it needed a huge amount of work doing to it. That was when my property maintenance course came into play for the first time. Cath and I, together with Kieran, Naomi and her parents, worked tirelessly over the next three months to get the house into a liveable state. It all came together in the end and Kieran and Naomi were very happy there – until they had to move again a couple of years later.

In the March of 2009 an unexpected opportunity arose. I was going to the gym with Fags when I met Lieutenant Commander Matt Grindon, who had been a Test Pilot at Boscombe with us but was now the Commanding Officer of 848 Squadron. He asked if I would come and work on 848, as the squadron was short of experienced A2 instructors and needed help. I explained to Matt that Tim Kelly, the RNR manpower organiser and staff officer, had said I was too old and was not able to get signed on as a reservist. Matt and the head of the Air Branch, Commander Steve Chain, had managed to reverse that decision so I could now join the RNR Air Branch as an aircrewman, which was fantastic for me. A part-time job, not employed on a regular basis, still flying, working when I wanted to – and this still gave me the ability to ski instruct and do all the sporty things I had done as a service regular.

Cath was happy for me to join so I applied the next week and because my aircrew medical was still in date, I could join as soon as the paperwork was completed. As with lots of bureaucratic societies, it takes longer than you think to complete any application and to that end, it was not until June that I was re-enlisted in the RN as a reservist. I joined again as a Warrant Officer 1 Aircrewman and went straight on to 848 Squadron to carry out my refresher training on the Sea King Mk4 in the commando role.

It was nice to be back in to the Naval fold and flying again, but the added benefit was that as a Warrant Officer 1 reservist I had no real leadership or divisional responsibilities within the squadron. When I went into work, I planned, briefed, flew, debriefed, did some sport and then went home. A perfect day – and they were paying me to do this, deep joy! After a while another reservist, POACMN Spike Hughes, and I had to do our examination to requalify as A2 instructors, after a ground and air trap/examination with George Gardiner the Standards WO, we were all spammed up and fully employable as instructors on the squadron.

Life was pretty good. Michelle had given birth to another child in January 2011, a lovely little girl called Isla, our fourth grandchild, two boys and two girls. Then came a bit of a setback not long after Isla was born: Simon decided he didn't love Michelle anymore, so he and Michelle split up and decided to get divorced. Ryan was nearly four and Isla not long born. Michelle left and moved back to Stevenage where her mother lives, she got a job teaching at a private school near Stevenage and bought a place on the outskirts of the town. We still see Ryan and Isla often and they are growing up into lovely young people.

I had now been on 848 for some time and while sitting in the Aircrewman's crew room, the lads were chatting about when they had joined the RN/RM. They were talking and spinning dits and stories, I think the oldest of them was 30 years old and had joined the Navy in 2000. When one asked me when I'd joined, I said September 1968; there was a pregnant pause then one lad exclaimed that his mum wasn't even born then. That made me feel quite old!

In 2012 the Olympic Games were held in London and as part of their commitment the squadron had to deploy a flight of Sea Kings to cover security for the period before, during and after the Olympics. The training flying still had to go on though, so Spike and I were employed for a nine-week period as regulars; this meant going into work each day during that time – which was a bit of a shock to the system, having to get up every morning and go to work. I could see why retirement was so nice and why I didn't want a full time job.

On 1 September I got airborne to go on a low-level navigation exercise down in Dartmoor; the sortie lasted two hours and thirty minutes, I needed only fifteen minutes to achieve my 8,000 hours, a milestone that previously I thought I would never achieve. On landing back at the squadron, the aircrew came out to the aircraft with a wheel chair and wheeled me back to the squadron, where I was covered in flour and water, cheered for my achievement and presented with a bottle of Pussers rum, on the front of which the squadron aircrewmen had engraved a set of aircrewman's wings and 8,000 hours. It was a wonderful gift and to this day I have not yet opened the bottle.

Around the same time, it also came to pass that I was playing squash with John Fagan and, you guessed it, for the first time in all the years we had been playing, he beat me three games to two. Fags always put it down to his dear departed father, who had said, 'John, one day you will beat him.'

So, I got my 8,000 hours and Fags won his game of squash.

Chapter 18

It was now 2012, and 21 November marked forty years since my first flight as aircrew in the Royal Navy. I had planned to fly on that day, but obviously the word had got out and as we landed in front of 848 Squadron hangar, a reception party came out to meet me and escort me into the hangar, as I went through the vast doors to the hangar I could see half the squadron there, also Cath, Kieran and Simon. The press was there too and to meet me was the Commanding Officer of CHF Captain Matt Briers RN. He made a speech and then presented me with a pen and ink drawing of all the types of aircraft I had flown in over the previous forty years. It was a fantastic surprise, which I know had been set up by John Fagan. In fact, it was he who had commissioned the drawing, which was a wonderful gesture and it now hangs in pride of place in my hallway for all to see. It is a one off and I truly thank him for it.

The next year started normally, with some skiing at the Royal Navy Ski Championships in Tignes, France, and some part time RNR flying. Then in the April of 2013, I was due my annual aircrew medical. I went for my pre-examination ECG, weight, hearing and eyesight test, then to the medical itself. I had passed all the normal tests but my ECG report showed a pulse of 47 which is low, but for me was pretty normal. The doctor said that this was not normal for a man of my age and there could be a problem. I said I thought it was normal for a man who is quite fit, still cycles, plays squash and golf a lot. She thought that quite insolent, so she grounded me. I was gobsmacked and flabbergasted that after all these years, this was the first time I had ever been grounded from an annual medical.

I then had to go and see a Consultant Cardiologist at Taunton hospital and go through a series of tests: a twenty-four hour ECG, a twenty-four hour blood pressure test, a series of tests on my heart – even though the consultant said there was nothing wrong with me. Eventually, after a year, I had to go to RAF Henlow, to the RAF Centre of Aviation Medicine, to have a stress

ECG, which involved twenty minutes on a treadmill while wired up to an ECG machine. After thirty minutes on the treadmill the operator told me all looked fine to him and I was good to go. When I then went to see a Wing Commander Doctor, he said it looked OK but that one heartbeat in thirty minutes of testing fell below the datum line; I had failed the test. He even explained that 60 per cent of the tests were in error, but I could not take the test again. I would have to have a CT angiogram, either in London or Oxford, to confirm that nothing was wrong. A month later I was in the CT scanning machine at the John Radcliffe Hospital in Oxford having my angiogram. Two weeks later the principal medical officer at Yeovilton called me in to give me my results.

Guess what? There was nothing wrong with me and I could go back flying. What a waste of time and effort, nearly eighteen months out of the job I loved and probably with no way back into aviation because my currency had lapsed.

I was still in the RNR and kept on working at the squadron on the ground, and even more so with John Fagan in the tasking role at CHF HQ. One good thing did happen though: I was offered a job with Mario Carretta, an ex-boss and test pilot from Boscombe Down. The role was as a civilian working for a company called PRIZM. We were to go out to New Zealand and help the NZ Air Force with the development of their practices, procedures and techniques for their new helicopter, the Eurocopter NH90, a medium/heavy battlefield troop aircraft. I jumped at the chance, having always wanted to go to New Zealand. Cath was OK with it, even more so when I told her the pay was good and after a six-week working period, she could fly out and we would have a three-week holiday touring North and South Islands of NZ.

The six weeks of work in NZ was great, working with the Kiwis was an eye-opener. Their techniques were slightly different to ours, but that's not to say they were wrong, just different. The aircraft was very good; in fact I thought this would have been a fine replacement for the Sea King, rather than the larger Merlin, which forces in the UK were about to move to.

At the end of October Cath arrived in Wellington, after a thirty-six hour trip from home. I had hired a car and we started our NZ tour with a night in Wellington, then over to the South Island, circumnavigating around via Christchurch, Dunedin, Queenstown and Nelson, sampling the wine, food and scenery. The South Island was simply stunning and I would recommend anyone to go and see it for themselves if possible. Rolling hills, snow-capped mountains, deep valleys, and glaciers that were once massive, but are now gradually being eroded away by the warming planet. Vineyards abounded which produce some of the best white wine I have ever tasted. Well worth the visit if you like a bit of wine tasting. A great holiday after working for the Kiwis who were some of the nicest people you could meet, generous and good hearted.

In April Mario contacted me again to ask if I was available to go to New Zealand for more work; we would work again out of 3 Squadron at Ohakia as we had done before; I was happy with this as long as it finished by the end of May, so it didn't clash with plans Cath and I had made to travel to Canada with her sister Marion in June. I devised a plan that I would fly back from Auckland via Los Angeles to Toronto and meet them there.

The work with the Kiwis this time involved Special Forces operations, inserts and extractions, these would take place in the centre of Auckland, just by the Sky Tower in the centre of the city at night on NVG. The Kiwis did well, they needed a few tips but the training and operational capability assessment was all good. After a while writing reports, it was time for me to leave and meet up with Cath and Marion. The flight to LA was uneventful, but the trip to Toronto was delayed slightly and subsequently Cath and Marion arrived in Canada way before me. On arrival in Toronto I picked up a hire car and drove in to town; after cruising around a while I saw two women sitting on a wall outside the hotel Cath had booked, I parked up and realised the women were actually Cath and Marion. Later that week when we met with my nephew Liam, Cath told him where we had stayed and he exclaimed that it was the red-light district. Cath and Marion joked about being a little miffed; they had sat on the wall for about forty minutes waiting for me and had not once been approached for any trade!

We got back home in July and I returned to work to discover that the Sea King would be phased out early and that my flying career had finally come to an end. My last flight had taken place in New Zealand; a special forces hit at night on Night Vision Goggles, to the ASB Building next to the Sky Tower, not a bad flight with which to end your forty-three-year flying career. I was still in the Naval Reserve, I had a job at CHF HQ, plus I had been signed on until the day before my 65th birthday. The job was fine, it still meant that I could ski instruct during the winter, do my cricket stewarding at Lords and the Oval during the summer and keep working with Fags for a few more years.

Life was good; Kieran was now the commanding officer of 26 Regiment Royal Artillery and Simon was the Director of Sports at Perrot Hill Prep School and had a new partner, Becky, who was also a teacher. Cath was playing more golf for the Ladies at Yeovil golf club and I had bought lots of woodworking equipment with the pay I had accrued in NZ. It looked like my Naval employment would come to an end, but then I found out I had been signed on yet again, for another two years. Now I would leave the Naval reserves on 1 January 2020. This means that having joined the RN in 1968 and leaving the Reserves in 2020, I had served just over fifty-one years. Not a bad career, a life in the service that gave me fulfilment, enjoyment, professional gratification, sporting experiences, world travel and most of all the best bunch of mates and working peers anyone in their wildest dreams could hope for. I would not have changed my career for anything. What a life and the most supportive person in my life and my career has been my wife Cath. She never complained (much) while I was away, be it on detachment or away during conflicts at the far corners of the earth. She was my rock and the stability for my family life, looking after Kieran and Simon.

The first of January 2020 was the last day of my military career, the end of an era for me, but one that I would not have swapped for anything. During my life and flying career, I have used up all of my nine lives and maybe even some more. I have been so lucky to have survived, while others have not been so fortunate. Some of my friends have died, too many to name, but I think of them all, every time I attend the Remembrance Day commemorations at the Cenotaph in November and say a few words for them. They are gone but not forgotten.

The advert for the Royal Navy fits me perfectly:
'Born in Nottingham, made in the Royal Navy.'

List of Abbreviations

A109	Augusta 109 Attack Helicopter
AAC	Army Air Corps
AB	Able Seaman
ACA	Aircrewmans Association
ASAP	As soon as possible
ASW	Anti-Submarine Warfare
AT	Adventurous Training
Banyan	Beach BBQ and Drinks
BERC	British Electrical Resistance Company
BFT	Basic Flying Training
C17	US Built Cargo Aircraft
CDO	Commando
Cdr	Commander RN
CHF	Commando Helicopter Force
Cpl	Corporal
CPO	Chief Petty Officer
CPOACMN	Chief Petty Officer Aircrewman
CRAB	Nickname for the RAF by the RN and Army
DIT	Naval or War story
Drafter	Aircrewman Job Appointer
DSM	Distinguished Service Medal
DZ	Drop Zone
E&E	Escape and Evasion
ETPS	Empire Test Pilots School
FAA	Fleet Air Arm
FCPO	Fleet Chief Petty Officer
Fish Head	An RN General Service sailor
FOB	Forward Operating Base
GPMG	General Purpose Machine Gun

COMMANDO HELICOPTER AIRCREWMAN

HMS	Her Majesty's Ship
IRA	Irish Republican Army
IRI	Instrument Rating Instructor
JEM	Junior Electrical mechanic
JEM(A)	Junior Electrical mechanic (Air)
Junglie	A person who has served on a Commando Squadron
KGB	Russian Intelligence Service
KKMC	King Khalid Military City
Knot	One nautical mile per hour
LAX	Los Angeles Airport
LEM	Leading Electrical Mechanic
LH	Leading Hand
LP	landing Point
LPH	Landing Platform helicopter
LSL	Landing Support Logistics Ship
Lt	Lieutenant
Lt Cdr	Lieutenant Commander RN
LZ	Landing Zone
M&AW	Mountain and Arctic Warfare Cadre
Maj	Major
MAOT	Mobile Air Operations Team
MCT	Maritime Counter Terrorism
MILEX	Military Training Exercise
Mk	Mark
MSR	Main Supply Route
NAAFI	Navy, Army, and Air Force Institute
NACS	Naval Air Commando Squadron
NASU	Naval Aircraft Support unit
NAV	Navigation
NBC	Nuclear, Biological and Chemical
NI	Northern Ireland
NVG	Night Vision Goggles
OCF	Operational Conversion Flight
OCU	Operational Conversion Unit or Course
OFT	Operational Flying Training
OP	Observation Post
PAN	Precautionary Emergency Radio Call
PO	Petty Officer
POACMN	Petty Officer Aircrewman

LIST OF ABBREVIATIONS

PoW	Prisoner of War or Prince of Wales
PT	Presentation Team
Pussers/Andrew	Royal Navy
QAI	Qualified Aircrew Instructor
QHI	Qualified Helicopter Instructor
QHTI	Qualified Helicopter Tactics Instructor
RAF	Royal Air Force
RFA	Royal Fleet Auxiliary
RM	Royal Marines
RN	Royal Navy
RNAF	Royal Norwegian Air Force
RNAS	Royal Naval Air Station
RR	Rolls Royce
RSM	Regimental Sergeant Major
RUC	Royal Ulster Constabulary
RV	Rendezvous Point
SAR	Search and Rescue
SAS	Special Air Service
SBS	Special Boats Section
SF	Special Forces
Sgt	Sergeant
SONAR	Sound Ranging
SULB	Single Use Lift Bag
TAG	Telegraphist Air gunner
TANS	Tactical Air Navigation System
Up, Up, Up	Emergency Call to climb
USMC	United States Marine Corps
USS	United States Ship
VCP	Vehicle Check Point
VOR, DME, ADF	Navigation Aids
WAFU	Wet and F---ing Useless. Nickname for a Fleet Air Arm Rating or for real, Weapons and Fuel Usage
WO	Warrant Officer
WRNS	Womens Royal Naval Service

Index

154

INDEX

INDEX